the organic DOG BISCUIT COOKBOOK

3rd Edition

FROM THE

Bubba Rose
BISCUIT COMPANY

FULLY **REVISED** UPDATED EDITION

HUMAN TESTED • ANIMAL APPROVED

CIDER MILL PRESS
BOOK PUBLISHERS

KENNEBUNKPORT, MAINE

13-Digit ISBN: 978-1-64643-139-7
10-Digit ISBN: 1-64643-139-1

This book may be ordered by mail from the publisher. Please include $5.99 for postage and handling. Please support your local bookseller first!

Books published by Cider Mill Press Book Publishers are available at special discounts for bulk purchases in the United States by corporations, institutions, and other organizations. For more information, please contact the publisher.

Cider Mill Press Book Publishers
"Where good books are ready for press"
12 Spring Street
PO Box 454
Kennebunkport, Maine 04046

Visit us online
cidermillpress.com

Design by Jessica Disbrow
Printed in China

2 3 4 5 6 7 8 9 0

ACKNOWLEDGMENTS

To all the people who made this book possible, we want to say a huge thank you!

A love of dogs has led to a lifelong career making dogs and their people happy and I can't thank everyone who supported and continues to support us enough.

And of course to Bob (aka Bubba) and Rose, my beloved first dogs; without them I wouldn't have done any of this. They have both since passed, but not a day goes by I don't think of them and continue to strive to make our products better. Their legacy always lives on in our name and inspiration.

PHOTO: JANET ZAPPASODI

TABLE OF CONTENTS

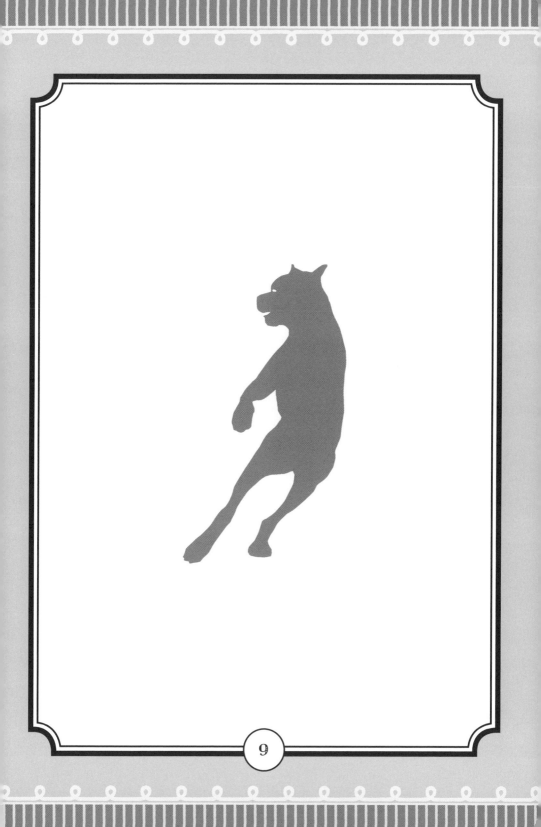

INTRODUCTION

The Bubba Rose Biscuit Company was founded out of a desire to give our dogs healthier treats. Dogs are family. Period. We believe that every dog treat should be made with real, wholesome, clean ingredients. That's why we use local, organic, fresh ingredients from the USA and never any preservatives. Every treat we bake is corn, soy- & gluten-free (the most common allergens and fillers in commercial products) and always baked in small batches in our bakery in FL. All our meats are locally sourced, free-range, grass-fed, and hormone- and antibiotic-free. We only use local cage-free eggs as well. We love animals (that includes farm animals) and want only the best quality and most humane meat & eggs being used in our treats. Everything we make is free of chemicals, salt, artificial flavors, colors, fillers and GMO ingredients. Just healthy, simple ingredients go into our treats. And by the way, the dogs absolutely love them! We thought everyone deserved to have their own recipes that followed these principles so they could whip up homemade treats for their favorite four-legged friends too. Dogs do know the difference with these homemade treats, we're certain of it. So try them out! There are lots of recipes in this book to choose from, and we guarantee your dog will be happy you put forth the effort.

{ IT'S ORGANIC }

With people spending more time and energy to find out where their food comes from and how it is made, it's natural that their focus should turn, too, to wanting to know more about what they feed their pets. I am careful about what I eat and where my food comes from, which led us to do the same for my dogs, especially in light of so many large-scale pet food recalls. After thoroughly researching the options, I feed my dogs a rotation diet of kibble, canned and raw food made from organic produce, and hormone and antibiotic-free meats. We use these same principles when we create the recipes that we use for our complete line of dog treats sold throughout the US and all over the world, as well as the recipes included in this book. Treats shouldn't just taste good, they should be good for them too.

There are so many organically grown and manufactured products out there to choose from. So you should have no problem finding the best ingredients from which to make your treats. And if you do run into a problem finding an organic ingredient listed in any of these recipes, you can always swap it out for its non-organic counterpart (do try to find a quality alternative, though). Your homemade treats aren't being certified, so do your best to make them with top-notch ingredients and your dogs will love you for it. We promise!

{ WHEAT-, CORN-, & SOY-FREE }

Every recipe in this book is free of wheat, corn and soy—the most common sources of food allergies in dogs. We know that dogs love treats so much they'll eat them regardless of the fact that the ingredients might make them itchy or not feel well afterward. But avoiding these ingredients and still producing healthy, tasty treats is not hard—as you'll see in all these recipes! By using the recipes in this book, you can take pride in knowing your dogs (and any dog to whom you give these treats) will be happier and healthier.

{ THE PANTRY LIST }

This is a list of the dry ingredients used most frequently in the recipes in this book. Keeping them stocked and handy will make it easy for you to bake a fresh, quality treat for your dog any day of the week. Please choose to use organic when you can. We do!

Oat flour
Brown rice flour
Oat bran
All-natural peanut butter (or peanuts to grind your own; it's easy)
Honey
Applesauce (unsweetened)
Wild-caught canned tuna and salmon

{ STOCK THE FRIDGE & FREEZER }

Besides the dry ingredients listed prior, here are a few items to have on hand in your refrigerator (or to keep frozen in the freezer) so you'll have them whenever you want to make treats. As always, please choose to use organic when you can.

Shredded cheddar cheese (It saves time.)
Grated Parmesan cheese
Organic eggs
Bacon (This works especially well if you cook and drain it, then freeze it, so there is always some on hand when the mood strikes to bake homemade dog treats.)
Chicken, turkey, and beef
(The next time you are cooking any of these for your dinner, cook some without any seasonings or sauces, grind it in a food processor, and then freeze so you'll have the pre-cooked meat ready to use in your baking.)

{ SUBSTITUTIONS }

Baking dog biscuits is not rocket science. Things can easily be exchanged, added, or omitted, depending on what you have available or what your dog particularly likes. These recipes are all very easily adjustable. If you are making substitutions, just keep an eye on the dough consistency when mixing. If it's too dry, add more water. Too wet, add more flour. It's pretty simple. For instance, if a recipe calls for turkey, and you have chicken on hand, go for it! Or if a recipe calls for blueberries and your dog loves raspberries, swap them! Just keep an eye on the baking time. If they are browning faster than the time says, remove them from the oven. If they still look too light, add a few more minutes and keep an eye on them. Your dogs will love most things you make for them, so know they'll be happy even if you think you over- or under-cooked the treat a bit. Remember, your dog will love a tasty homemade treat and appreciate the effort.

A common substitution people email us about that's worth mentioning is the replacement of eggs in any of the recipes. All dough needs a binding agent to hold it together, and we use eggs. Most dogs are fine with the one egg used in each recipe, though some dogs do have allergies to them. If your dog is allergic to eggs, here are some substitutions you can try:

1 medium to small banana = 1 egg
3 tablespoons applesauce (use unsweetened) = 1 egg

But please keep in mind that they are not exactly the same as an egg would be, so add the liquid portion of the recipe slowly since it may take more or less due to the difference in moisture these substitutes add.

Another common substitution people look for are different flour options, either as a result of what they can find in their local store, or what they have already in their pantry. We choose to use a combination of organic oat flour and organic brown rice flour, as we tried lots of flour combinations (since it can be a bit tricky working with non-wheat flours) and liked this one best, but there are lots of options. We created all our recipes to be wheat-, corn-, and soy-free, and recommend you use a wheat-free flour if you have the opportunity, as it is such a common dog allergy these days. Here are a few other wheat-free flour choices you can use if you have any difficulty with the ones we are using:

Amaranth flour
Arrowroot flour
Barley flour
Buckwheat flour (it's not really wheat)
Chickpea (or garbanzo bean) flour
Millet flour
Potato flour
Quinoa flour
Tapioca flour

When you swap a flour in the recipes with one of these or another one you have purchased, use the same amount of total flour that the recipe calls for, but add the liquid portion slowly since it may take more or less moisture due to the substitution. And, interesting fact, flour can hold up to 40% of it's weight in moisture, so humidity or lack thereof can greatly affect the amount of liquid your recipe needs to come together to a usable consistency.

{ TOOLS OF THE TRADE }

The following is a list of utensils and kitchen tools used in many of the recipes in this book; we highly recommend them. If you don't have them, there are alternatives to use, or you can mix and stir by hand. But from experience, we can say that the easier these are to make, the better. The more effort and mess that goes into these treats, the less likely you are going to want to make them again.

ROLLING PIN

So many of these recipes require you to roll out the dough before cutting it with either a cookie cutter, knife, pizza cutter or upside-down glass. You can cut the dough with many different items, but you really need the rolling pin to flatten the dough. They make nonstick rolling pins, which are a nice investment (you really don't want tuna in your next batch of cookies). But if you don't have one, to prevent the dough from sticking to your rolling pin (which happens since a lot of these doughs are a little sticky to work with) we recommend using a large plastic food-grade storage bag and placing it on top of your lightly floured dough—then roll away. It works like a charm.

FOOD PROCESSOR

This truly is your kitchen wonder tool. You can use the grinding attachments to puree liver, make your own peanut butter, chop the cooked vegetables and meats down to fine pieces, etc. Besides, once you've finished the prep work, you switch to your dough attachment and let the machine mix the dough for you. You will still need to scrape the sides, but it cuts down on so much of the work you'll need to do. In our opinion, every kitchen should have one.

PARCHMENT PAPER

This makes clean-up a breeze. You don't want liver in the corners of your good cookie or jelly roll pans, do you? If you line your normal baking pans with a sheet of parchment paper first, all you have to do is peel it off and toss it when you're done.

CUTTING MAT

We love the thin, plastic dishwasher-safe ones. Besides cutting and prepping your food on them, they are flexible, so you can curl them and slide all your ingredients directly into the mixing bowl.

LATEX GLOVES

Some of the ingredients in the treats can be slightly unpleasant to work with. Who wants to mix a dough with tuna or liver in it and risk the smell permeating your hands when you work with it? Throw on a pair of disposable latex gloves (any supermarket carries them in their cleaning aisle) and work away.

COOKING PANS

This book contains a lot of recipes that use your standard cookie sheet or jelly roll pan. Some flat pan is probably necessary. There are also some recipes that require a muffin pan, mini muffin pan, mini loaf pans and square baking pans. If you don't have any of these, you can always skip that recipe and pick one for which you do have the pans—or substitute with something you have on hand. If you choose an alternate pan, know that you will need to keep an eye on the baking times, as they differ with the different thicknesses of the doughs or mixtures you are using.

{ STORAGE TIPS }

Remember these recipes are all for homemade, preservative-free treats. With that in mind, they can't sit out the way processed dog treats can. We recommend storing them in a plastic bag or container in the refrigerator. Even in there they will still mold, like your leftovers, so store only an amount you think you will use within a week. Any extras (since these recipes yield more than a week's worth of treats for most households) can be frozen to thaw out later (this works great) or given away as gifts to your friends, neighbors or coworkers. Homemade dog biscuits are a great item to share and a perfect gift for the dog lovers in your life. Dogs should definitely be in on the goodness, so spread the happiness! They make great gifts for the holidays too!

If you are looking to keep the treats on the counter, in your pocket for training, etc., and want to make sure they stay fresh for your pup, you will need to make sure you cook them nice and crispy. Thinner is better for this. If the cookies are cut thinner they will cook more quickly and get crispier, allowing them to stay fresh longer without refrigeration. Add a few more minutes to your cook time, to make sure they are crispy, and allow them to cool and air out over night, to really ensure the moisture is out of them before you move them to another container. Again, please keep in mind, we cannot know what the moisture levels are in the treats you make yourself, therefore we can not tell you a specific amount of time they can maintain freshness out of the fridge. But a general rule of thumb is thinner is better, crispier is necessary, and it's safer to stay with the non-meaty recipes for this purpose.

{ YIELDS }

We tried to make these recipes as simple as possible and recommend using whatever you have on hand to form the shapes of the treats. That said, we can not state precisely how many treats each recipe will make. We also don't know your intended audience. If you have a Chihuahua, you'll obviously want to make smaller-sized treats (they'll also cook faster, so keep an eye on them). And if a Great Dane is your canine companion, make them larger (again, watch them, then they might need a little longer to cook). Most of the recipes are about the same size, so once you make one, you can anticipate how many treats you'll get out of it. Using a standard 3" or so cookie cutter, you can estimate 20-30 treats per batch and a little over one pound of treats.

{ SOFT OR CRUNCHY? }

You know your dogs and their tastes or dietary needs. If you want the treats to be softer, cook them a little less or on a lower heat (definitely keep them in the refrigerator, too). If you want your treats to be a little harder, cook them longer at a lower heat. Or, when they are finished cooking, turn the oven off but leave them in there on the tray to cool for a few hours or overnight. Remember, this is all supposed to be an easy and fun thing to do for your beloved dogs. If they don't turn out perfectly, I bet your dogs won't mind one bit and will be so happy you made something special for them anyway.

CHAPTER 1

FORGET-ME-NOTS

A special treat for your favorite four-legger for each month of the year

Life without celebrations would be no fun at all, right? Dogs are lucky in that they need nothing more than our very presence to find cause for celebration. Still, occasions marked with particularly yummy treats soon become particularly special for them. When dogs see that turkey being stuffed for Thanksgiving, they know leftovers are imminent. Boxes of chocolates that appear for Valentine's, Easter, and other holidays signal to them that something special is happening (we've included recipes that provide safe options so your dogs will no longer be robbed of these delicacies).

When all is said and done, if there is an event worth celebrating with family and friends, there's no reason not to include something special for your four-legged family member. Here are 12 recipes to correspond with a significant celebration in every month of the year.

Choose to use organic ingredients in these recipes, like we do!

BLACK & WHITE COOKIES

Usher in the New Year on the right paw. If you're staying home and enjoying a festive dinner with family and friends, consider going black tie to transform the evening into a memorable, formal affair. Dogs look great with their tuxes and tails on, too, and when they greet your guests at the door looking spiffy with a black bow-tie or tiara on, everyone will know there's a party goin' on. Watch that your guests don't go for these scrumptious-looking black-and-white cookies; they'll be tempted!

FOR THE DOUGH:

1 ½ c. oat flour

1 ½ c. brown rice flour

½ c. peanut butter (unsalted)

1 tbsp. honey

1 egg

½ c. water (add slowly)

FOR THE TOPPING:

8 oz. carob chips (do not substitute with chocolate)

8 oz. white chocolate chips (these are safe for dogs)

Preheat oven to 350°. Combine all dough ingredients (except the water) together. Add water slowly and mix until a dough forms (if too dry, add more water, too wet, add a bit more flour). You may not need all the water if you reach a good consistency first. Roll out on a lightly floured surface to ¼" thickness. Use a round cookie cutter or the rim of an upside down glass to cut out 2" circles in the dough. Line a cookie sheet with parchment paper (for easy cleanup), and place the cookies on the sheet (they can be rather close together as they don't grow much while cooking).

Bake 20-25 minutes or until golden brown. Transfer and let cool completely on a wire rack.

When the cookies are cooling, prepare the topping. To do so, heat the white chocolate chips over low heat in a double boiler or in the microwave until melted. Dip half of each cookie into the melted white chocolate and place back on a wire rack to cool. Once all cookies are cooled, at least to the touch, heat the carob chips in a double boiler or in the microwave until melted. Dip the other half of each cookie into the melted carob and place back on a wire rack to cool.

Store the cookies in an airtight container in the refrigerator. For additional options, read the "Storage Tips" section on page 18.

LITTLE SWEETHEARTS

At this time of year when it's appropriate to go over-the-top in displaying your affection, go ahead and really shower it on your dog(s). With these healthy, red-colored, heart-shaped cookies, you can go ahead and spoil them knowing you won't be plying him with a lot of artificial ingredients. Natural food colorings are made from plants and vegetables and readily available in any health food store or online.

1 ½ c. oat flour

1 ½ c. brown rice flour

½ c. grated parmesan cheese

6-oz. can tomato paste

1 tsp. basil

1 egg

½ c. water (add slowly)

Natural red food coloring (optional)

Preheat oven to 350°. Combine all dough ingredients (except the water) together. Add enough red food coloring to reach the desired color. Add water slowly and mix until a dough forms (if too dry, add more water, too wet, add a bit more flour). You may not need all the water if you reach a good consistency first. Use a heart-shaped cookie cutter (or a knife) to cut out shapes. Roll out on a lightly floured surface to $1/4$" thickness. Line a cookie sheet with parchment paper (for easy cleanup), and place the cookies on the sheet (they can be rather close together as they don't grow much while cooking).

Bake 20-25 minutes or until golden brown. Transfer and let cool completely on a wire rack. Store the cookies in an airtight container in the refrigerator. For additional options, read the "Storage Tips" section on page 18.

NATURAL FOOD COLORINGS

Beets are the source of a lot of the red natural food colorants. You can change the color of the dough with these other natural colorants for other occasions. Remember, though, that these fruits and vegetables add flavor, too. Use sparingly to be sure your dog will like it and so you don't overpower the other flavors. Also, never use coffee or any kind of grape juice to add color (or flavor) to a recipe as these ingredients are harmful to dogs.

BLUEISH-PURPLE: Blueberries, Red cabbage
PURPLE: Blackberries
RED: Beets, Tomatoes
PINKISH-RED: Beets, Strawberries, Hibiscus
GREEN: Spinach, Kale
YELLOWISH-ORANGE: Turmeric, Curry powder
ORANGE: Annatto

IRISH WOLFHOUNDERS

On St. Patrick's Day—March 17—everyone is Irish for the day. Your preferred method of celebration may be to have a green bagel or beer. We don't recommend that you share that particular tradition with your dog, but you can be assured they'll stay close by your bar stool if you have a plate of these with you. And you know what? They taste pretty good with beer, so you may want to nibble on them, too.

1 ½ c. oat flour

1 ½ c. brown rice flour

1 ½ c. tightly packed spinach leaves

½ c. shredded cheddar cheese

½ c. grated parmesan cheese

2 tbsp. rosemary

½ c. oat bran

1 egg

½ c. water (add slowly)

Preheat oven to 350°. Puree the spinach leaves in a food processor until smooth. Combine all ingredients (except the water) together. Add water slowly and mix until a dough forms (if too dry, add more water, too wet, add a bit more flour). You may not need all the water if you reach a good consistency first. Roll out on a lightly floured surface to ¼" thickness. Use a shamrock-shaped cookie cutter (or a knife) to cut out shapes. Line a cookie sheet with parchment paper (for easy cleanup), and place the cookies on the sheet (they can be rather close together as they don't grow much while cooking).

Bake 20-25 minutes or until golden brown. Transfer and let cool completely on a wire rack. Store the cookies in an airtight container in the refrigerator. For additional options, read the "Storage Tips" section on page 18.

ROSEMARY

Rosemary is an excellent antioxidant and full of vitamin C, vitamin A, iron, folic acid, dietary fiber, and potassium. It is a natural antibiotic and antiseptic and is known to have anti-inflammatory, anti-allergic, and anti-fungal properties. It supports immune system functions and defends against free radical damage.

HOPALONGS

For all you hound people out there, you know the thrill that the mention of the Easter Bunny brings for many of your dogs. Is there anything better than ol' Peter Cottontail's fresh scent in the hedgerow? Well, for those deprived of the Real Thing, these treats will surely come in a close second; in fact, they may even keep your super-sniffer away from the stash of goodies you're trying to hide from you-know-who. While you're making these, remember, spring is just around the corner!

FOR THE CAKE:

2 ½ c. oat flour

3 eggs

½ c. honey

2 tsp. baking powder

½ tsp. baking soda

1 tsp. cinnamon

2 c. pureed carrots

¼ c. safflower oil

1 tsp. vanilla

FOR THE FROSTING:

8-oz. package low-fat cream cheese (at room temperature)

2 tbsp. honey

———≫———•———≪———

Preheat oven to 350°. Peel and dice the carrots, then puree the carrot pieces in a food processor.

Combine the carrots with all the other ingredients in a large bowl and mix thoroughly. Place cupcake papers in a mini muffin pan (or a regular muffin pan). Spoon mixture evenly into the papers, filling close to the top (the mix will not rise very much).

Bake 10-15 minutes if using the mini muffin pan or 20-25 minutes if using a regular-sized muffin pan. Cupcakes are done when a toothpick inserted in the center comes out clean. Let cool completely on a wire rack.

Combine frosting ingredients together and whip until well mixed and fluffy. Decorate the cupcakes. Store the cupcakes in an airtight container in the refrigerator. For additional icing options, view the other icing recipes on pages 169 and 171.

———≫———•———≪———

SUNFLOWER POWER

The days are getting longer and warmer; the flowers are blooming; spring has sprung. Celebrate the joy of a new season with these special cookies, infused with a healthy dose of sunflower seeds, cranberries and oats—how perfect!

1 ¼ c. oat flour

1 ¼ c. brown rice flour

1 c. hulled sunflower seeds (unsalted)

½ c. rolled oats (the old-fashioned kind, not instant)

½ c. dried cranberries

¼ c. honey

3 tbsp. applesauce (unsweetened)

1 egg

½ c. water (add slowly)

Preheat oven to 350°. Set aside ½ c. sunflower seeds to use for topping. Combine all other ingredients (except the water) together. Add water slowly and mix until a dough forms (if too dry, add more water, too wet, add a bit more flour). You may not need all the water if you reach a good consistency first. Roll out on a lightly floured surface to ¼" thickness. Use a flower-shaped cookie cutter (or a knife) to cut into shapes. Line a cookie sheet with parchment paper (for easy cleanup), and place the cookies on the sheet (they can be rather close together as they don't grow much while cooking).

Bake 20-25 minutes or until golden brown. Transfer and let cool completely on a wire rack. Store the cookies in an airtight container in the refrigerator. For more options, read the "Storage Tips" section on page 18.

OATS

Oats contain a higher concentration of protein, calcium, iron, magnesium, zinc, copper, manganese, thiamin, folacin, and vitamin E than any other unfortified whole grain (such as wheat, barley, corn, etc.). They are high in fiber, amino acids, and lipids, which contain a good balance of essential fatty acids for overall good health. Oats are a grain with a low gluten content. They have been shown to lower cholesterol and reduce the risk of heart disease.

GRILLIN' AND CHILLIN'

Get out the barbeque, summertime is here! While you're enjoying classic summer dishes like BBQ chicken, ribs, sausages, and burgers paired with potato salad and other goodies, it just wouldn't be right not to have something equally scrumptious and appropriate for your dog. These cookies are like cheeseburgers with all the fixings— including a dose of healthy sesame seeds and parsley (in fact, you may want to try adding these to your burgers!).

1 $\frac{1}{2}$ c. oat flour

1 $\frac{1}{2}$ c. potato flour

$\frac{1}{2}$ c. shredded low-fat cheddar cheese

$\frac{1}{2}$ c. lean ground beef (pre-cooked and drained)

6-oz. can tomato paste

1 tbsp. dried parsley

1 egg

$\frac{1}{2}$ c. water (add slowly)

2 tbsp. sesame seeds (save for topping)

Preheat oven to 350°. Cook and drain ground beef. Combine all ingredients (except the water and sesame seeds) together. Add water slowly and mix until a dough forms (if too dry, add more water, too wet, add a bit more flour). You may not need all the water if you reach a good consistency first. Form into hamburger shaped patties (about 2" in diameter). Line a cookie sheet with parchment paper (for easy cleanup), and place the cookies on the sheet (they can be rather close together as they don't grow much while cooking). Sprinkle them with the sesame seeds.

Bake 22-27 minutes or until golden brown. Transfer and let cool completely on a wire rack. Store the cookies in an airtight container in the refrigerator. For more options, read the "Storage Tips" section on page 18.

PARSLEY

Parsley's role as an attractive garnish has long since been replaced by that of a nutritious and delicious health benefit. Parsley is loaded with vitamins A, B, C, and K and the minerals calcium, potassium, iron, magnesium, phosphorous, as well as protein. It is high in chlorophyll, which gives it the natural freshening power associated with combating foul-smelling breath. All these things make it a great addition to a dog's diet.

RED, WHITE, AND OL' BLUE

It's fun to make a cake that looks like the American flag with strawberries and blueberries on the 4th of July, but these sensational fruits can—and should—be enjoyed all month. Their benefits are available for your dog, too, in these fruit-filled, naturally sweetened cookies.

1 $\frac{1}{4}$ c. oat flour

1 $\frac{1}{4}$ c. brown rice flour

$\frac{1}{2}$ c. oat bran

$\frac{1}{2}$ c. strawberries (fresh or frozen)

$\frac{1}{2}$ c. blueberries (fresh or frozen)

2 tbsp. honey

1 tsp. cinnamon

1 egg

$\frac{1}{4}$ c. water (add slowly)

Preheat oven to 350°. Puree strawberries and blueberries in a food processor. Combine all ingredients (except the water) together. Add water slowly and mix until a dough forms (if too dry, add more water, too wet, add a bit more flour). You may not need all the water if you reach a good consistency first. Roll out on a lightly floured surface to ¼" thickness. Use any fun patriotic-shaped cookie cutter (or a knife) to cut into shapes. Line a cookie sheet with parchment paper (for easy cleanup), and place the cookies on the sheet (they can be rather close together as they don't grow much while cooking).

Bake 20-25 minutes or until golden brown. Transfer and let cool completely on a wire rack. Store the cookies in an airtight container in the refrigerator. For more options, read the "Storage Tips" section on page 18.

BERRIES

Several of the recipes in this chapter call for various berries, including cranberries, blueberries, and strawberries. Wonder no longer, all are safe for dogs. Berries are natural antioxidants; in fact, recent studies have shown that blueberries are especially rich in them. Cranberries are known for relieving urinary tract infections and promoting uterine health. Berries also contain lots of vitamin C. They are naturally sweet and tasty, and dogs really enjoy them. They can be served fresh, frozen, or dried.

PAWLICKIN' CHICKEN

Did you know that late July through mid August are considered the "dog days of summer"? Well we say let's break the heat with these tasty BBQ chicken treats that your dog will be sure to go crazy for. With all those barbecues in full swing by now, why not treat your favorite four-legged friend to their very own chicken treat.

1 ¼ c. oat flour

1 ¼ c. brown rice flour

½ c. ground chicken (cooked)

½ c. oat bran

1 tbsp. blackstrap molasses

2 tbsp. tomato paste

1 tsp. apple cider vinegar

1 egg

½ c. water

Preheat oven to 375°. Combine all ingredients (except the water) together. Add water slowly and mix until a dough forms (if too dry, add more water, too wet, add a bit more flour). You may not need all the water if you reach a good consistency first. Roll out on a lightly floured surface to $\frac{1}{4}$" thickness. Use any shaped cookie cutter (or a knife) to cut into shapes. Line a cookie sheet with parchment paper (for easy cleanup), and place the cookies on the sheet (they can be rather close together as they don't grow much while cooking).

Bake 22-27 minutes or until golden brown. Transfer and let cool completely on a wire rack. Store the cookies in an airtight container in the refrigerator. For more options, read the "Storage Tips" section on page 18.

AVOID THE ONIONS

We rely on onions to add flavor to many of our summer favorites, and it's often included in barbeque sauces. They don't harm us (though raw onions make for bad breath), but they have been shown to cause damage to dogs' red blood cells, which can lead to anemia. It's best to avoid all forms of onion in the food you give your dogs—raw, cooked, and even powdered onion.

AUTUMN APPLE CRISPS

Apples are wonderful for everyone, dogs included! There's nothing like a crisp, juicy apple to signal the beginning of fall. You can feed your dog pieces of raw apple as a snack (they love to crunch them just like we do), or cook the apples down into a soft sauce (no sugar!) and add a spoonful or two to their meals. This recipe brings out the great flavor of apples with some cheddar cheese and honey—a recipe no dog can resist!

1 ½ c. oat flour

1 ½ c. brown rice flour

1 tsp. cinnamon

1 c. applesauce (unsweetened)

½ c. rolled oats (the old-fashioned kind, not instant)

1 tbsp. honey

1 egg

½ c. water

Preheat oven to 350°. Combine all ingredients (except the water) together. Add water slowly and mix until a dough forms (if too dry, add more water, too wet, add a bit more flour). You may not need all the water if you reach a good consistency first. Roll out on a lightly floured surface to $1/4$" thickness. Use an apple-shaped cookie cutter (or a knife) to cut into shapes. Line a cookie sheet with parchment paper (for easy cleanup), and place the cookies on the sheet (they can be rather close together as they don't grow much while cooking).

Bake 20-25 minutes or until golden brown. Transfer and let cool completely on a wire rack. Store the cookies in an airtight container in the refrigerator. For more options, read the "Storage Tips" section on page 18.

PUMPKIN BITES

As you're preparing costumes for yourself, your kids, and your dog(s) for the magical day of Halloween, look for recipes that include pumpkin—that super-nutritious vegetable that is the centerpiece of so many Halloween and fall celebrations. For yourself and your family, make a pumpkin soup or pumpkin bread. For your dog, make these Pumpkin Bites. With your tummies full, you'll be ready to turn your attention to carving the most glorious pumpkins.

1 ½ c. oat flour

1 ½ c. brown rice flour

½ c. pumpkin (canned or fresh)

2 tbsp. molasses (regular or blackstrap)

1 tsp. cinnamon

1 tsp. ground ginger

1 tbsp. honey

1 egg

Preheat oven to 350°. Combine all ingredients (except the water) together. Add water slowly and mix until a dough forms (if too dry, add more water, too wet, add a bit more flour). You may not need all the water if you reach a good consistency first. Roll out on a lightly floured surface to 1/4" thickness. Use a pumpkin-shaped cookie cutter (or a knife) to cut into shapes. Line a cookie sheet with parchment paper (for easy cleanup), and place the cookies on the sheet (they can be rather close together as they don't grow much while cooking).

Bake 22-27 minutes or until golden brown. Transfer and let cool completely on a wire rack. Store the cookies in an airtight container in the refrigerator. For more options, read the "Storage Tips" section on page 18.

PUMPKIN, YAMS, SWEET POTATOES

Sweet potatoes and yams are high in potassium and beta carotene (a natural antioxidant) and low in calories. They are also soothing for an upset stomach. Did you know that a tablespoon of canned or fresh sweet potatoes, yams, or pumpkin on top of your dog's food will help to regulate an upset stomach?

ALL THE FIXINS

This is our favorite time of the year, and as the big Thanksgiving feast is being prepared, dogs get excited, too. They see lots of food being made, family and friends getting together, tables being set for a special feast—and they want to share in the good times and good eats. Save the fatty gravy and skins that can lead to digestive upset in dogs for yourself (and maybe give that a little consideration too), and make these cookies, which are like a Thanksgiving meal in a cookie—irresistible, and healthy.

½ c. pureed carrots

½ c. cooked, mashed sweet potatoes (or yams)

1 ½ c. oat flour

1 ½ c. brown rice flour

½ c. ground turkey (cooked)

2 eggs

½ c. dried cranberries

2 tbsp. honey

1 tsp. dried rosemary

1 tsp. ground cinnamon

Preheat oven to 375°. Peel and dice carrots. Place in a food processor and puree. Cook and mash sweet potatoes. Combine all ingredients together and mix until a dough forms. Roll out on a lightly floured surface to ¼" thickness. Use any shaped cookie cutter (or a knife) to cut into shapes. Line a cookie sheet with parchment paper (for easy cleanup), and place the cookies on the sheet (they can be rather close together as they don't grow much while cooking).

Bake 22-27 minutes or until golden brown. Transfer and let cool completely on a wire rack. Store the cookies in an airtight container in the refrigerator. For more options, read the "Storage Tips" section on page 18.

CRANBERRIES

Cranberries are an antioxidant-rich super fruit. They are a good source of vitamin E, vitamin K, dietary fiber, vitamin C and manganese. The polyphenols, antioxidants and flavonoids in cranberries have been found to have beneficial qualities for kidney, bladder and urinary tract health, dental health and gum disease, cardiovascular health and improvements in age-related declines of memory, balance and coordination in animals.

GINGERBREAD MAILMEN

For so many, the holiday season comes alive through baking. The kitchen becomes a place to create special cookies, breads, preserves—goodies that make friends and family feel special and welcomed, and that can be wrapped in festive papers to create the perfect gift. Absolutely no holiday celebration would be complete without the gingerbread man. Now your favorite four-legged family member gets their very own.

1 ½ c. oat flour

1 ½ c. brown rice flour

1 tsp. cinnamon

1 tsp. ground ginger

1 tsp. ground cloves

1 egg

¼ c. blackstrap molasses

¼ c. peanut butter (unsalted)

1 tbsp. apple cider vinegar

½ c. water

Preheat oven to 350°. Combine all ingredients (except the water) together. Add water slowly and mix until a dough forms (if too dry, add more water, too wet, add a bit more flour). You may not need all the water if you reach a good consistency first. Roll out on a lightly floured surface to $1/4"$ thickness. Use a gingerbread man shaped cookie cutter (or any cookie cutter) to cut into shapes. Line a cookie sheet with parchment paper (for easy cleanup), and place the cookies on the sheet (they can be rather close together as they don't grow much while cooking).

Bake 20-25 minutes or until golden brown. Transfer and let cool completely on a wire rack. Store the cookies in an airtight container in the refrigerator. For more options, read the "Storage Tips" section on page 18.

These are a great treat to decorate and give out to all the dogs on your holiday lists. There are some icing recipes on pages 169 and 171 that can be used with this recipe to make some truly special treats for your the four-legged family members this holiday season.

CHAPTER 2

SANDWICH BOARD

The daily specials—all the classics

Don't you love going into one of those classic American diners and finding a sandwich menu that's several pages long and includes some one-of-a-kind concoctions? It makes your mouth water just to consider the possibilities! So imagine how your dog will feel when he gets to sample from this menu. If you have several of these flavor varieties on hand, you can even let him choose his favorite for the day—just as you do at the diner!

Choose to use organic ingredients in these recipes, like we do!

SAVORY CHICKEN

{ SAGE AND CHICKEN, WHAT A COMBO }

1 ½ c. oat flour

1 ½ c. brown rice flour

½ c. ground chicken (cooked)

½ c. oat bran

1 tsp. ground sage

1 egg

½ c. chicken broth (add slowly)

Preheat the oven to 350°. Combine all ingredients (except the broth) together. Add broth slowly and mix until a dough forms (if too dry, add more broth, too wet, add a bit more flour). You may not need all the water if you reach a good consistency first. Use a cookie cutter (or a knife) to cut into shapes. Roll out on a lightly floured surface to ¼" thickness. Line a cookie sheet with parchment paper (for easy cleanup), and place the cookies on the sheet (they can be rather close together as they don't grow much while cooking).

Bake 22-27 minutes or until golden brown. Transfer and let cool completely on a wire rack. Store the cookies in an airtight container in the refrigerator. For more options, read the "Storage Tips" section on page 18.

BROTH VS. GRAVY

Like the recipes in the cookbooks you use, the ones here feature ingredients that you would normally purchase from a store. One of these is chicken broth (or beef or vegetable broth). If you want to really spoil your dog (and the rest of your family), you can make these broths at home, then refrigerate them so you have them handy to use in your recipes. A broth is essentially the juice that's created when meat or vegetables are steamed or boiled. Don't substitute gravy, which is a broth-based food that's had other things mixed into it to thicken or stabilize it—usually cornstarch. Besides that, our recipes are corn-free, as the grain is a potential source of allergies in dogs.

BACON, EGG & CHEESE

{ THE BREAKFAST STAPLE FOR EVEYRONE }

1 1/2 c. oat flour

1 1/2 c. brown rice flour

1/2 c. shredded cheddar cheese

6 slices cooked bacon

2 eggs

1/4 c. water (add slowly)

Preheat the oven to 350°. Combine all ingredients (except the water) together. Add water slowly and mix until a dough forms (if too dry, add more water, too wet, add a bit more flour). You may not need all the water if you reach a good consistency first. Roll out on a lightly floured surface to 1/4" thickness. Use a cookie cutter (or a knife) to cut into shapes. Line a cookie sheet with parchment paper (for easy cleanup), and place the cookies on the sheet (they can be rather close together as they don't grow much while cooking).

Bake 22-27 minutes or until golden brown. Transfer and let cool completely on a wire rack. Store the cookies in an airtight container in the refrigerator. For more options, read the "Storage Tips" section on page 18.

BACON IS NOT ALL THE SAME

Not all things are created equal, and this definitely applies to bacon. It is the favorite breakfast side, as well as quite arguably the most desirable piece of piggie there is. With that being said, we do recommend that you purchase natural bacon, which is not raised with any antibiotics and is free-range and nitrite free. These characteristics make for a healthier treat and it definitely is tastier for you too! While you're cooking it up for these treats, give it a taste too. We are sure you'll notice the difference!

CHEESEBURGERS!

{ IT'S JUST A PLAIN OLD CHEESEBURGER – OH, SO TASTY }

1 ½ c. oat flour

1 ½ c. brown rice flour

1 egg

½ c. lean ground beef (pre-cooked and drained)

½ c. shredded low-fat cheddar cheese

¼ c. tomato paste

½ c. water

>>>> • <<<<

Preheat the oven to 350°. Combine all ingredients (except the water) together. Add water slowly and mix until a dough forms (if too dry, add more water, too wet, add a bit more flour). You may not need all the water if you reach a good consistency first. Roll out on a lightly floured surface to ¼" thickness. Use a round cookie cutter or the rim of an upside-down glass to cut into 2" circles. Line a cookie sheet with parchment paper (for easy cleanup), and place the cookies on the sheet (they can be rather close together as they don't grow much while cooking).

Bake 22-27 minutes or until golden brown. Transfer and let cool completely on a wire rack. Store the cookies in an airtight container in the refrigerator. For more options, read the "Storage Tips" section on page 18.

PREPARING THE BEEF

We ask that you precook the ground beef in this and other recipes in this book because it results in the safest end-product for your dog. Even if you start with organic, grass-fed beef (or other meat), you want to make sure that any harmful bacteria are cooked out and that you are draining as much of the fat off the cooked meat as possible before adding it to the other ingredients in these recipes.

TURKEY & SWISS

{ ... HOLD THE MAYO! }

1 ½ c. oat flour

1 ½ c. brown rice flour

½ c. grated Swiss cheese

½ c. ground turkey (pre-cooked and drained)

½ c. oat bran

1 tbsp. dried parsley

1 egg

½ c. water

Preheat the oven to 350°. Combine all ingredients (except the water) together. Add water slowly and mix until a dough forms (if too dry, add more water, too wet, add a bit more flour). You may not need all the water if you reach a good consistency first. Roll out on a lightly floured surface to ¼" thickness. Use a cookie cutter (or a knife) to cut into shapes. Line a cookie sheet with parchment paper (for easy cleanup), and place the cookies on the sheet (they can be rather close together as they don't grow much while cooking).

Bake 22-27 minutes or until golden brown. Transfer and let cool completely on a wire rack. Store the cookies in an airtight container in the refrigerator. For more options, read the "Storage Tips" section on page 18.

SUBSTITUTIONS, JUST DO IT!

The great thing about baking your own dog treats is that you can substitute many of the ingredients for items you have on hand or that you know your dog prefers. Since these flours are a little tricky to work with, I would avoid swapping those out as the recipe will require a good amount of adjusting with a different flour. But the main "flavor" ingredients can easily be switched around. For example, the above recipe calls for turkey and Swiss cheese. What if you have roast beef and provolone? Go ahead and use them instead. It's that easy throughout. If you want to swap tuna for salmon or chicken for turkey in a recipe, feel free. *Take note*, however: NEVER substitute an ingredient that may be toxic to dogs, such as onions, chocolate, raisins, macadamia nuts, or grapes.

CHEESE, PLEASE!

{ LOVED BY KIDS AND DOGS ALIKE }

1 ½ c. oat flour

1 ½ c. brown rice flour

1 c. shredded low-fat cheddar cheese

½ c. grated parmesan cheese

1 egg

½ c. water

Preheat the oven to 350°. Combine all ingredients (except the water) together. Add water slowly and mix until a dough forms (if too dry, add more water, too wet, add a bit more flour). You may not need all the water if you reach a good consistency first. Use a cookie cutter (or a knife) to cut into shapes. Roll out on a lightly floured surface to ¼" thickness. Line a cookie sheet with parchment paper (for easy cleanup), and place the cookies on the sheet (they can be rather close together as they don't grow much while cooking).

Bake 22-27 minutes or until golden brown. Transfer and let cool completely on a wire rack. Store the cookies in an airtight container in the refrigerator. For more options, read the "Storage Tips" section on page 18.

CHEESE IS ALWAYS A WINNER

Ok, so let's cut to the chase: dogs love cheese. It's a plain and simple fact; that's why so many people can use a slice of cheese to conceal their dog's medicine in (when it's necessary to give them it). We use cheese in a lot of our recipes, both in this book and in our product line for this very same reason. You can always exchange cheeses, too, with one you have on hand.

PUP PIZZA

{ NO CRUSTS HERE, THIS ONE'S ALL THEIRS }

FOR DOUGH:

1 ½ c. oat flour

1 ½ c. brown rice flour

1 egg

¼ c. low-fat ricotta cheese

⅓ c. water

FOR TOPPING:

6-oz. can tomato paste

1 c. shredded low-fat mozzarella cheese

1 tsp. dried basil

1 tsp. dried oregano

Preheat oven to 375°. Combine all the dough ingredients together and mix thoroughly until a dough forms. Roll out on a lightly floured surface to ¼" thickness. Use a round cookie cutter or the rim of an upside-down glass to cut 2" round circles out of the dough. Line a cookie sheet with parchment paper (for easy cleanup), and place the

cookies on the sheet (they can be rather close together as they don't grow much while cooking).

Now for the toppings. Spread the tomato paste on each first, then sprinkle the cheese and spices on top of each.

Bake 22-27 minutes or until golden brown. Transfer and let cool completely on a wire rack. Store the cookies in an airtight container in the refrigerator. For more options, read the "Storage Tips" section on page 18.

Alternates: For an extra twist, add a few slices of turkey or other low-fat pepperoni or diced grilled chicken on top of the pizzas before baking. Think of all those savory pizza toppings you love so much or use some of your dog's favorite meats on top for an extra special treat.

ARROZ CON POLLO

{ MUY BUENO! }

1 ¹/₂ c. oat flour

1 ¹/₂ c. brown rice flour

¹/₂ c. ground chicken (cooked)

¹/₂ c. cooked brown rice

1 tbsp. dried parsley

1 tbsp. paprika

1 egg

¹/₂ c. water (or chicken broth)

Preheat oven to 350°. Combine all ingredients (except the water) together. Add water slowly and mix until a dough forms (if too dry, add more water, too wet, add a bit more flour). You may not need all the water if you reach a good consistency first. Roll out on a lightly floured surface to ¹/₄" thickness. Use a cookie cutter (or a knife) to cut into shapes. Line a cookie sheet with parchment paper (for easy cleanup), and place the cookies on the sheet (they can be rather close together as they don't grow much while cooking).

Bake 22-27 minutes or until golden brown. Transfer and let cool completely on a wire rack. Store the cookies in an airtight container in the refrigerator. For more options, read the "Storage Tips" section on page 18.

FOR THE SCHOLARLY DOG

Before he just gobbles up these yummy treats, you may want to educate and inspire your dog by telling him what these Spanish words mean in English. It's so simple it only takes a second. *Arroz* means rice, and *pollo* means chicken. Arroz con pollo is rice with chicken, or more familiarly, chicken-and-rice. Lesson learned.

CHEESE FRIES

{ THE LATE-NIGHT CLASSIC }

1 ½ c. oat flour

1 ½ c. brown rice flour

1 tsp. baking soda

2 tsp. baking powder

1 c. shredded low-fat cheddar cheese

1 egg

¼ c. extra-virgin olive oil

½ c. water

Preheat the oven to 350°. Combine all ingredients (except the water) together, reserving ½ c. cheddar cheese for the topping. Add water slowly and mix until a dough forms (if too dry, add more water, too wet, add a bit more flour). You may not need all the water if you reach a good consistency first. Roll the dough out on a lightly floured surface. Separate pieces and form sticks (about 3" long and ½" in diameter). Line a cookie sheet with parchment paper (for easy cleanup), and place the cookies on the sheet (they can be rather close together as they don't grow much while cooking). Sprinkle the remaining cheddar cheese on top of the fries.

Bake 22-27 minutes or until golden brown. Transfer and let cool completely on a wire rack. Store the cookies in an airtight container in the refrigerator. For more options, read the "Storage Tips" section on page 18.

OILS

There are many kinds of oils available to cook with, and you may be tempted to use something other than extra-virgin olive oil. We list that kind of oil as an ingredient, however, because we feel that it is the kind that is best used by your dog's body. Most vegetable oils are soybean- or corn-based, and we prefer to use extra-virgin olive oil.

LIVER & BACON

{ GRANDPA'S FAVORITE—BUT NO ONIONS }

$^1/_2$ lb. raw beef or chicken livers

6 slices cooked bacon

1 $^1/_2$ c. oat flour

1 $^1/_2$ c. brown rice flour

1 c. oat bran

1 egg

$^1/_2$ c. water

Preheat oven to 375°. Puree livers in a food processor. Grind bacon into fine pieces in a food processor. Immediately clean the food processor afterward; you definitely don't want either of these pulverized meats drying in your appliance. Cleaning this up if they do is not easy.

Combine all ingredients (except the water) together. Add water slowly and mix until a dough forms (if too dry, add more water, too wet, add a bit more flour). You may not need all the water if you reach a good consistency first. Roll out on a lightly floured surface to $^1/_4$" thickness. Use a cookie cutter (or a knife) to cut into shapes. Line a cookie sheet with parchment paper (for easy cleanup), and place the

cookies on the sheet (they can be rather close together as they don't grow much while cooking).

Bake 22-27 minutes or until golden brown. Transfer and let cool completely on a wire rack. Store the cookies in an airtight container in the refrigerator. For more options, read the "Storage Tips" section on page 18.

Note: For crispier treats, do not take them out of the oven to cool. Turn the oven off and let them sit in there overnight. Store in the refrigerator once removed.

ONIONS—DEFINITELY A NO-NO

It has recently been reported that onions can be toxic (poisonous) to dogs (and cats). These foods have been shown to cause a form of hemolytic anemia in some animals who ingested them. Hemolytic anemia is a disease of the red blood cells. For this reason, we advise you not to use them in any of our recipes, or in any foods you prepare or give to your dog(s).

DUCK A LA KING

{ A SAVORY DUCK TREAT }

1 ½ c. oat flour

1 ½ c. brown rice flour

½ c. oat bran

½ c. ground duck breast (pre-cooked and drained)

1 tsp. rosemary

1 egg

½ c. water (add slowly)

Preheat the oven to 350°. Combine all ingredients (except the water) together. Add water slowly and mix until a dough forms (if too dry, add more water, too wet, add a bit more flour). You may not need all the water if you reach a good consistency first. Roll out on a lightly floured surface to ¼" thickness. Use a cookie cutter (or a knife) to cut into shapes. Line a cookie sheet with parchment paper (for easy cleanup), and place the cookies on the sheet (they can be rather close together as they don't grow much while cooking).

Bake 22-27 minutes or until golden brown. Transfer and let cool completely on a wire rack. Store the cookies in an airtight container in the refrigerator. For more options, read the "Storage Tips" section on page 18.

GAME BIRDS INSTEAD?

A lot of dogs these days are accustomed to eating some pretty delectable birds, including pheasant, duck, goose, quail, etc. If you happen to hunt or know a hunter and have easy access to these other delicious game birds, feel free to substitute the duck for any one of these meats instead. These are all great protein sources, as well as being less common, therefore making it less likely that there would be any built-in allergies to them.

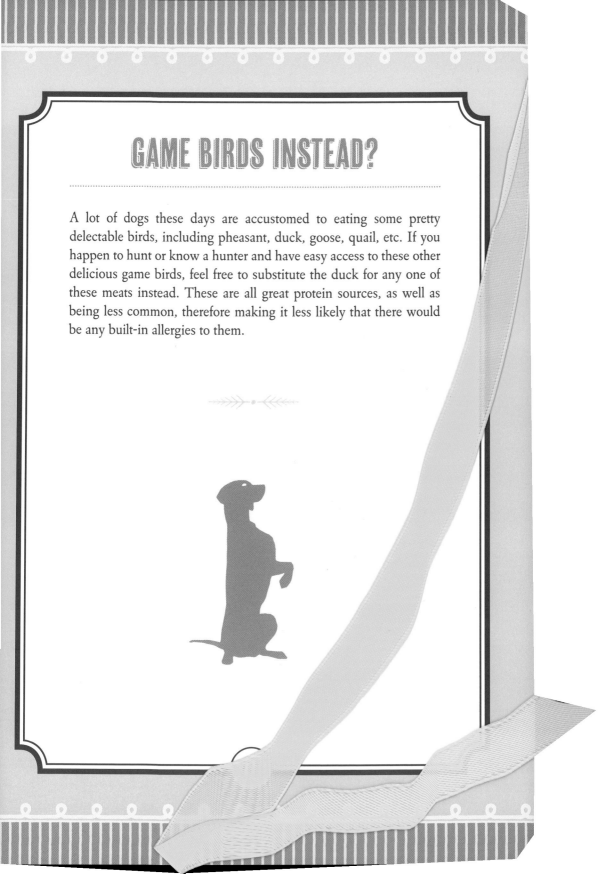

FISH & CHIPS

{ THE IRISH SETTER OF SNACK FOODS }

....

1 ½ c. oat flour

1 c. potato flour

½ c. oat bran

½ c. cod (or another white fish)

1 tsp. dill

1 egg

½ c. water (add slowly)

⟫⟩⟩→ • ←⟨⟨⟪

Preheat oven to 350°. Cook the cod thoroughly (use as little oil as possible). Finely grind it in a food processor.

Combine all ingredients (except the water) together. Add water slowly and mix until a dough forms (if too dry, add more water, too wet, add a bit more flour). You may not need all the water if you reach a good consistency first. Roll out on a lightly floured surface to ¼" thickness. Use a cookie cutter (or a knife) to cut into shapes. Line a cookie sheet with parchment paper (for easy cleanup), and place the cookies on the sheet (they can be rather close together as they don't grow much while cooking).

Bake 22-27 minutes or until golden brown. Transfer and let cool completely on a wire rack. Store the cookies in an airtight container in the refrigerator. For more options, read the "Storage Tips" section on page 18.

FISH FOR DOGS!

Everyone knows that fish is good for you, but why? And what about contaminants like mercury or other toxins? To answer the first question, fish is a rich source of important omega-3 fatty acids. These are the ones that support the optimal functioning of the heart, eyes, immune system, skeletal system, and skin and coat. Supplementing with omega-3-rich foods can benefit such conditions as allergies, arthritis, heart disease, and even cancer. Of course, it's important to find high-quality sources of fish so that its benefits aren't outweighed by what may be contaminating it—including mercury. That is why we recommend using wild-caught fish in our recipes.

DOGGIE DUMPLINGS

{ SOMETHING SPECIAL IN EVERY BITE! }

FOR DOUGH:

1 ½ c. oat flour

1 ½ c. brown rice flour

1 tsp. baking powder

1 egg

½ c. chicken broth

FILLING SUGGESTIONS:

Canned pumpkin

Cheese cubes (cheddar's always a favorite)

Small peeled apple pieces

Beef (cooked and ground or in small pieces)

Turkey (cooked and ground or in small pieces)

Bacon (cooked and crumbled)

Tuna

Peanut Butter (unsalted)

Preheat the oven to 350°. Combine all dough ingredients (except the water) together. Add water slowly and mix until a dough forms (if too dry, add more water, too wet, add a bit more flour). You may not need all the water if you reach a good consistency first. Roll out on a lightly floured surface to ¼" thickness. Use a round cookie cutter or the rim of an upside-down glass to cut 2 ½" circles. Place a small amount of any of the suggested fillings—or another of your dog's favorite things—in the center and press the edges up and together making a little bundle. Line a cookie sheet with parchment paper (for easy cleanup), and place the cookies on the sheet (they can be rather close together as they don't grow much while cooking).

Bake 25-30 minutes or until golden brown. Transfer and let cool completely on a wire rack. Store the cookies in an airtight container in the refrigerator. For more options, read the "Storage Tips" section on page 18.

GRILLED CHEESE WITH BACON

{ AN ALL-TIME FAVORITE }

1 ½ c. oat flour

1 ½ c. brown rice flour

½ c. shredded low-fat cheddar cheese

6 slices cooked bacon

1 egg

½ c. water

Preheat oven to 350°. Cook bacon slices, then finely grind them in a food processor.

Combine all ingredients (except the water) together. Add water slowly and mix until a dough forms (if too dry, add more water, too wet, add a bit more flour). You may not need all the water if you reach a good consistency first.

Roll out on a lightly floured surface to ¼" thickness. Use a cookie cutter (or a knife) to cut into shapes. Line a cookie sheet with parchment paper (for easy cleanup), and place the cookies on the sheet (they can be rather close together as they don't grow much while cooking).

Bake 22-27 minutes or until golden brown. Transfer and let cool completely on a wire rack. Store the cookies in an airtight container in the refrigerator. For more options, read the "Storage Tips" section on page 18.

MEAT & POTATOES

{ THAT'S PRONOUNCED MEAT AND POTATAS }

1 $\frac{1}{2}$ c. oat flour

1 $\frac{1}{2}$ c. potato flour

$\frac{1}{2}$ c. oat bran

$\frac{1}{2}$ c. lean ground beef (pre-cooked and drained)

1 tsp. parsley

1 tsp. oregano

1 tsp. basil

1 egg

$\frac{1}{2}$ c. water (add slowly)

Preheat the oven to 350°. Combine all ingredients (except the water) together. Add water slowly and mix until a dough forms (if too dry, add more water, too wet, add a bit more flour). You may not need all the water if you reach a good consistency first.

Roll out on a lightly floured surface to $\frac{1}{4}$" thickness. Use a cookie cutter (or a knife) to cut into shapes. Line a cookie sheet with parchment paper (for easy cleanup), and place the cookies on the sheet (they can be rather close together as they don't grow much while cooking).

Bake 22-27 minutes or until golden brown. Transfer and let cool completely on a wire rack. Store the cookies in an airtight container in the refrigerator. For more options, read the "Storage Tips" section on page 18.

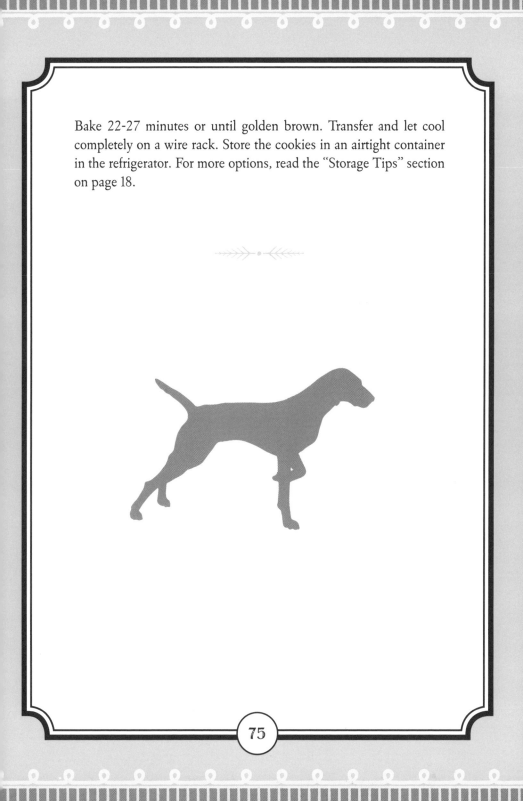

LIVER & CHEDDAR

{ GRANDMA'S FAVORITE }

1 c. raw chicken liver (or beef liver)

1 ½ c. oat flour

1 ½ c. brown rice flour

½ c. shredded low-fat cheddar cheese

1 egg

½ c. water (add slowly)

Preheat oven to 350°. Puree the liver in a food processor. Immediately clean the food processor afterward; once the liver dries it is very hard and unpleasant to get out of there.

Combine all ingredients (except the water) together. Add water slowly and mix until a dough forms (if too dry, add more water, too wet, add a bit more flour). You may not need all the water if you reach a good consistency first. Roll out on a lightly floured surface to ¼" thickness. Use a cookie cutter (or a knife) to cut into shapes. Line a cookie sheet with parchment paper (for easy cleanup), and place the cookies on the sheet (they can be rather close together as they don't grow much while cooking).

Bake 22-27 minutes or until golden brown. Transfer and let cool completely on a wire rack. Store the cookies in an airtight container in the refrigerator. For more options, read the "Storage Tips" section on page 18.

LIVER—IT'S TIME TO LOVE IT

Liver is an organ meat, and while all carnivores have been feasting on and benefiting from organ meats for as long as they've (we've) been roaming the planet, in the United States today, liver is much maligned as smelly and slimy. Add to that a reputation for being high in cholesterol, and it's no wonder it's not a popular choice for the family dinner table. But liver has long been an acceptable and desired ingredient in dog food and treats—and it's no wonder. Liver is loaded with vitamin A (retinol), which is good for your eyes, skin, and mucous membranes. It also contains vitamins E, D, and K, is packed with essential minerals, is a high-quality protein source, and is rich in omega-3 and omega-6 fatty acids. All these are great for your dog—and for you! One additional note: Because the liver is the detoxifying organ in the body, purchase meat that is as limited in its exposure to toxin-processing as possible, such as an organic cut.

BLACKSTRAP SNACKS

{ PECANS AND MOLASSES, WHAT'S NOT TO LOVE }

1 ½ c. oat flour

1 ½ c. brown rice flour

¼ c. finely ground pecans

½ c. rolled oats (old-fashioned kind, not instant)

¼ c. blackstrap molasses

1 egg

½ c. water (add slowly)

Preheat oven to 350°. Combine all ingredients (except the water) together. Add water slowly and mix until a dough forms (if too dry, add more water, too wet, add a bit more flour). You may not need all the water if you reach a good consistency first. Roll out on a lightly floured surface to ¼" thickness. Use a cookie cutter (or a knife) to cut into shapes. Line a cookie sheet with parchment paper (for easy cleanup), and place the cookies on the sheet (they can be rather close together as they don't grow much while cooking).

Bake 22-27 minutes or until golden brown. Transfer and let cool completely on a wire rack. Store the cookies in an airtight container in the refrigerator. For more options, read the "Storage Tips" section on page 18.

BENEFITS OF MOLASSES

If you're looking for alternative sources of sweeteners in a wide range of foods, one of the ones you should consider is blackstrap molasses. This thick syrup is the by-product of refining sugar: It is the third boiling of the sugar syrup, so it is technically the concentrate left over after the sugar's sucrose has been crystallized. What's left are lots of beneficial minerals—iron, copper, manganese, magnesium, potassium, and calcium—as well as a dose of vitamin B6. While the taste of blackstrap molasses takes some getting used to (though baked beans or ginger snaps wouldn't be the same without it), dogs are typically less discriminating. Ours love the flavor, and we're sure yours will, too.

BEEF BARLEY

{ A SOUP FAVORITE IN BISCUIT FORM }

1/2 c. pureed carrots

1/2 c. pureed celery

2 c. oat flour

1 1/2 c. barley flour

1/2 c. lean ground beef (pre-cooked and drained)

1/2 c. oat bran

1 tsp. parsley

1 tsp. dill

1 egg

1/2 c. water (add slowly)

Preheat oven to 350°. Peel and dice carrots and celery, then puree in a food processor.

Combine all ingredients (except the water) together. Add water slowly and mix until a dough forms (if too dry, add more water, too wet, add a bit more flour). You may not need all the water if you reach a good consistency first. Roll out on a lightly floured surface to 1/4" thickness. Use a cookie cutter (or a knife) to cut into shapes. Line a cookie sheet with parchment paper (for easy cleanup), and place the cookies on the sheet (they can be rather close together as they don't grow much while cooking).

Bake 22-27 minutes or until golden brown. Transfer and let cool completely on a wire rack. Store the cookies in an airtight container in the refrigerator. For more options, read the "Storage Tips" section on page 18.

BENEFITS OF BARLEY

Like wheat, barley is a grain that produces seeds that are then ground to produce flour. The benefits of barley compared to wheat include: barley is higher in fiber, contains vitamin E, and has more thiamin, riboflavin, lysine, and essential fatty acids.

SALMON ROLL

{ MAKE THIS SUSHI FAVORITE AN EASY TREAT }

1 ½ c. oat flour

1 ½ c. brown rice flour

6-oz. can wild-caught salmon

½ c. oat bran

1 tsp. dill

½ c. low-fat cream cheese

1 egg

½ c. water (add slowly)

Preheat oven to 350°. Combine all ingredients (except the water) together. Add water slowly and mix until a dough forms (if too dry, add more water, too wet, add a bit more flour). You may not need all the water if you reach a good consistency first. Roll out on a lightly floured surface to ¼" thickness. Use a cookie cutter (or a knife) to cut into shapes. Line a cookie sheet with parchment paper (for easy cleanup), and place the cookies on the sheet (they can be rather close together as they don't grow much while cooking).

Bake 22-27 minutes or until golden brown. Transfer and let cool completely on a wire rack. Store the cookies in an airtight container in the refrigerator. For more options, read the "Storage Tips" section on page 18.

SALMON

Salmon is low in calories and saturated fat, while high in protein. It is a wonderful source of the amazingly beneficial omega-3 fatty acids, vitamin D, selenium, B vitamins, and magnesium, which are excellent for skin, coat and heart health. And salmon is a great alternative protein source for dogs with allergies to the more common proteins of chicken and beef.

TUNA MELT

{ FRIES NOT INCLUDED }

1 ½ c. oat flour

1 ½ c. brown rice flour

½ c. oat bran

6-oz. can albacore tuna (in water)

½ c. shredded low-fat cheddar cheese

1 egg

¼ c. water (add slowly)

Preheat oven to 350°. Pour entire contents of can of tuna (including all water and juices) into a food processor and finely grind.

Combine all ingredients (except the water) together. Add water slowly and mix until a dough forms (if too dry, add more water, too wet, add a bit more flour). You may not need all the water if you reach a good consistency first.

Roll out on a lightly floured surface to ¼" thickness. Use a cookie cutter (or a knife) to cut into shapes. Line a cookie sheet with parchment paper (for easy cleanup), and place the cookies on the sheet (they can be rather close together as they don't grow much while cooking).

Bake 22-27 minutes or until golden brown. Transfer and let cool completely on a wire rack. Store the cookies in an airtight container in the refrigerator. For more options, read the "Storage Tips" section on page 18.

CHAPTER 3

SILVER PLATTER

For dogs who live in the lap of luxury

The recipes in Chapter 2 were created for that down-home kind of feeling—comfort food with a kick. These recipes—while equally delicious—are for the more adventurous palate, or to be served to canine friends of your too-classy pooch on special occasions (and let's face it, every day with your dog is a special occasion!). We hope you enjoy making and giving these to you dog as we did. *Bon appetit!*

Choose to use organic ingredients in these recipes, like we do!

THE APPETIZER

{ THE BEST IS ALWAYS THE CHEESY BREAD }

1 $\frac{1}{2}$ c. oat flour

1 $\frac{1}{2}$ c. brown rice flour

1 tsp. baking soda

2 tsp. baking powder

1 tsp. dried rosemary

$\frac{1}{2}$ c. grated parmesan cheese

1 egg

$\frac{1}{4}$ c. olive oil

$\frac{1}{2}$ c. water (add slowly)

$\frac{1}{2}$ c. low-fat shredded mozzarella cheese

———>>> • <<<———

Preheat oven to 350°. Set the mozzarella cheese aside to be used later as a topping. Combine all other ingredients (except the water) together. Add water slowly and mix until a dough forms (if too dry, add more water, too wet, add a bit more flour). You may not need all the water if you reach a good consistency first. Roll out on a lightly floured surface to $\frac{1}{4}$" thickness.

Use a cookie cutter (or a knife) to cut into shapes. Line a cookie sheet with parchment paper (for easy cleanup), and place the cookies on the sheet (they can be rather close together as they don't grow much while cooking). Sprinkle the mozzarella cheese on top of the cookies.

Bake 20-25 minutes or until golden brown. Transfer and let cool completely on a wire rack. Store the cookies in an airtight container in the refrigerator. For more options, read the "Storage Tips" section on page 18.

QUATTRO FORMAGGIO

{ WHEN ONE CHEESE JUST ISN'T ENOUGH }

1 ½ c. oat flour

1 ½ c. brown rice flour

½ c. grated parmesan cheese

½ c. low-fat ricotta cheese

½ c. shredded low-fat milk mozzarella

½ c. grated romano cheese

1 tsp. dried basil

1 tsp. dried oregano

1 egg

½ c. water

Preheat oven to 350°. Combine all ingredients (except the water) together. Add water slowly and mix until a dough forms (if too dry, add more water, too wet, add a bit more flour). You may not need all the water if you reach a good consistency first. Roll out on a lightly floured surface to ¼" thickness.

Use a cookie cutter (or a knife) to cut into shapes. Line a cookie sheet with parchment paper (for easy cleanup), and place the cookies on the sheet (they can be rather close together as they don't grow much while cooking).

Bake 22-27 minutes or until golden brown. Transfer and let cool completely on a wire rack. Store the cookies in an airtight container in the refrigerator. For more options, read the "Storage Tips" section on page 18.

ROTISSERIE CHICKEN

{ A SAVORY AND DELISH TREAT FOR ANY DOG }

1 1/2 c. oat flour

1 1/2 c. brown rice flour

1/2 c. ground chicken (cooked)

1 tbsp. rosemary

1 tbsp. sage

1 tbsp. grated parmesan cheese

1 egg

1/2 c. chicken broth (add slowly)

Preheat oven to 350°. Combine all ingredients (except the water) together. Add water slowly and mix until a dough forms (if too dry, add more water, too wet, add a bit more flour). You may not need all the water if you reach a good consistency first. Roll out on a lightly floured surface to 1/4" thickness.

Use a cookie cutter (or a knife) to cut into shapes. Line a cookie sheet with parchment paper (for easy cleanup), and place the cookies on the sheet (they can be rather close together as they don't grow much while cooking).

Bake 22-27 minutes or until golden brown. Transfer and let cool completely on a wire rack. Store the cookies in an airtight container in the refrigerator. For more options, read the "Storage Tips" section on page 18.

LICKIN' THEIR CHOPS FOR CHICKEN

Chicken is an ingredient in many dog foods, and for good reason. Besides being a protein that dogs eat, it is one of the best meat sources of protein. It also packs a good dose of amino acids and is easily digestible. Like other meat sources, it's important to select the finest cuts from the best sources to optimize the nutritional benefits. With the good, there is also the bad. Unfortunately, more dogs are becoming allergic to chicken, as it is so common in so many foods. If your dog is allergic to chicken, feel free to swap turkey, duck or any other protein into any of the recipes that call for chicken.

SOUTHWESTERN SIZZLER

{ A SIZZLING STEAK TREAT FOR ALL }

1 $\frac{1}{2}$ c. oat flour

1 $\frac{1}{2}$ c. brown rice flour

$\frac{1}{2}$ c. lean ground beef (pre-cooked and drained)

1 $\frac{1}{2}$ c. tightly packed spinach leaves

1 tbsp. sesame seeds

$\frac{1}{4}$ tsp. paprika

1 egg

$\frac{1}{2}$ c. water (add slowly)

Preheat oven to 350°.

Combine all ingredients (except the water) together. Add water slowly and mix until a dough forms (if too dry, add more water, too wet, add a bit more flour). You may not need all the water if you reach a good consistency first. Roll out on a lightly floured surface to $\frac{1}{4}$" thickness. Use a cookie cutter (or a knife) to cut into shapes. Line a cookie sheet with parchment paper (for easy cleanup), and place the cookies on the sheet (they can be rather close together as they don't grow much while cooking).

Bake 22-27 minutes or until golden brown. Transfer and let cool completely on a wire rack. Store the cookies in an airtight container in the refrigerator. For more options, read the "Storage Tips" section on page 18.

SUBSTITUTIONS ABOUND

Just a little reminder that we've already been over, but in case you missed it or forgot. Substitutions! Feel free to swap out the beef for another protein. Maybe your dog just doesn't digest beef all that well, just like a lot of people. Beef can be a bit tough to digest (leading to that all too well-known stinky butt). If that happens to your dog, then we recommend swapping out the beef for an alternative protein, such as venison or bison (which tend to be a lot better for those with beef sensitivities). Also, say you have kale in the fridge; you can use that instead of the spinach. Always keep in mind not to substitute with anything toxic to dogs, but there are a lot of options for quick and easy switches that you can do with what you have on hand.

CROCK-POT CLASSIC

{ A LITTLE BIT OF THIS, A LITTLE BIT OF THAT }

$\frac{1}{2}$ c. ground chicken (cooked)

$\frac{1}{2}$ c. ground pork (cooked)

6 slices cooked bacon

1 $\frac{1}{2}$ c. oat flour

1 $\frac{1}{2}$ c. brown rice flour

$\frac{1}{2}$ c. applesauce (unsweetened)

1 tsp. sage

$\frac{1}{2}$ c. grated parmesan cheese

2 eggs

$\frac{1}{4}$ c. water

Preheat oven to 350°. Finely grind the chicken, pork and bacon in a food processor.

Combine all ingredients (except the water) together. Add water slowly and mix until a dough forms (if too dry, add more water, too wet, add a bit more flour). You may not need all the water if you reach a good consistency first. Roll out on a lightly floured surface to $^1/_4$" thickness. Use a cookie cutter (or a knife) to cut into shapes. Line a cookie sheet with parchment paper (for easy cleanup), and place the cookies on the sheet (they can be rather close together as they don't grow much while cooking).

Bake 22-27 minutes or until golden brown. Transfer and let cool completely on a wire rack. Store the cookies in an airtight container in the refrigerator. For more options, read the "Storage Tips" section on page 18.

THE COUNTRY CLUB

{ TEE OFF ON THIS DELICIOUS THREE-PAR COMBO OF APPLE, CHEDDAR AND BACON }

6 slices cooked bacon

1 ½ c. oat flour

1 ½ c. brown rice flour

½ c. shredded low-fat cheddar cheese

½ c. applesauce (unsweetened)

½ c. rolled oats (old-fashioned kind, not instant)

1 egg

⅓ c. water

Preheat oven to 350°. Finely grind the bacon in a food processor.

Combine all ingredients (except the water) together. Add water slowly and mix until a dough forms (if too dry, add more water, too wet, add a bit more flour). You may not need all the water if you reach a good consistency first.

Roll out on a lightly floured surface to ¼" thickness. Use a cookie cutter (or a knife) to cut into shapes. Line a cookie sheet with parchment paper (for easy cleanup), and place the cookies on the sheet (they can be rather close together as they don't grow much while cooking).

Bake 22-27 minutes or until golden brown. Transfer and let cool completely on a wire rack. Store the cookies in an airtight container in the refrigerator. For more options, read the "Storage Tips" section on page 18.

MAMBO ITALIANO

{ OF COURSE IT'S GOT ROSEMARY! }

....

½ c. pureed roasted red peppers (optional)

1 ½ c. oat flour

1 ½ c. brown rice flour

6-oz. can tomato paste

½ c. fresh mozzarella, finely chopped

½ c. grated parmesan cheese

1 tsp. dried rosemary

1 tsp. dried oregano

1 tsp. dried basil

1 egg

½ c. water (add slowly)

Preheat oven to 350°. If using roasted red peppers, puree these in a food processor before doing anything else.

Combine all ingredients (except the water) together. Add water slowly and mix until a dough forms (if too dry, add more water, too wet, add a bit more flour). You may not need all the water if you reach a good consistency first. Roll out on a lightly floured surface to ¼" thickness. Use a cookie cutter (or a knife) to cut into shapes. Line a cookie sheet with parchment paper (for easy cleanup), and place the cookies on the sheet (they can be rather close together as they don't grow much while cooking).

Bake 22-27 minutes or until golden brown. Transfer and let cool completely on a wire rack. Store the cookies in an airtight container in the refrigerator. For more options, read the "Storage Tips" section on page 18.

ROSEMARY—FOR MORE THAN JUST SEASONING

Rosemary—like sage and thyme—is traditionally used to season foods, particularly roasted meats and vegetables. It is becoming more and more appreciated for its medicinal as well as gustatory benefits. Rosemary is a natural antibiotic and antiseptic. It also increases blood flow to the brain, aiding in memory and, when inhaled, rejuvenating the senses. It is a potent herb, and a little goes a long way—we could all use a little more often, though.

SESAME-CRUSTED
TUNA

{ IT'S SO WILD IT JUMPS OUT OF YOUR DISH }

6-oz. can wild-caught tuna

$^1/_2$ c. tightly packed arugula leaves

1 $^1/_2$ c. oat flour

1 $^1/_2$ c. brown rice flour

$^1/_2$ c. sesame seeds

$^1/_2$ c. finely ground peanuts

1 tbsp. honey

1 egg

$^1/_2$ c. water (add slowly)

Preheat oven to 350°. Empty entire contents of tuna can (including liquid and juices) into a food processor and puree it along with the arugula leaves.

Combine all ingredients (except the water) together. Add water slowly and mix until a dough forms (if too dry, add more water, too wet, add a bit more flour). You may not need all the water if you reach a good consistency first. Roll out on a lightly floured surface to $1/4"$ thickness. Use a cookie cutter (or a knife) to cut into shapes. Line a cookie sheet with parchment paper (for easy cleanup), and place the cookies on the sheet (they can be rather close together as they don't grow much while cooking).

Bake 22-27 minutes or until golden brown. Transfer and let cool completely on a wire rack. Store the cookies in an airtight container in the refrigerator. For more options, read the "Storage Tips" section on page 18.

NUTS—LET'S EXPLORE

Many of the recipes in this book contain peanuts, because what dog doesn't love peanut butter? Ok, we've heard of a few, but they are definitely in the minority. Other nuts that are good for dogs (and people) include cashews and almonds. Nuts are an excellent source of protein. But keep in mind that they are also high in fat. One nut to never feed your dog is the macadamia nut. While the exact source of its toxicity is still not known, it is associated with producing muscle tremors and partial paralysis in dogs. If you're going to get nutty, go for the good ones.

CABIN BY THE LAKE

{ A LITTLE FLAXSEED TO ENHANCE YOUR DOG'S NATURAL BEAUTY }

1 ½ c. oat flour

1 ½ c. brown rice flour

½ c. flaxseed meal (or flaxseeds)

½ c. ground peanuts (unsalted)

½ c. dried cranberries

3 tbsp. sesame seeds

1 egg

½ c. water (add slowly)

Preheat oven to 350°. Combine all ingredients (except the water) together. Add water slowly and mix until a dough forms (if too dry, add more water, too wet, add a bit more flour). You may not need all the water if you reach a good consistency first. Roll out on a lightly floured surface to ¼" thickness. Use a cookie cutter (or a knife) to cut into shapes. Line a cookie sheet with parchment paper (for easy cleanup), and place the cookies on the sheet (they can be rather close together as they don't grow much while cooking).

Bake 22-27 minutes or until golden brown. Transfer and let cool completely on a wire rack. Store the cookies in an airtight container in the refrigerator. For more options, read the "Storage Tips" section on page 18.

FLAXSEEDS

The seeds of the flax plant have been cultivated for human consumption for millennia. Flaxseed contains lignans, which are particularly beneficial to the female reproductive system. The fiber in flaxseed acts as a natural laxative to aid in digestion; in the intestine, it helps coat the lining, reducing the incidence of constipation, gastritis, and colon conditions. Using ground flaxseed in recipes certainly adds beneficial fiber and digestive support.

THE NOVA SCOTIA SPECIAL

{ THE UPTOWN WAY TO START THE DAY }

4 oz. lox

1 ½ c. oat flour

1 ½ c. brown rice flour

4 oz. low-fat cream cheese (at room temperature)

½ c. oat bran

1 tsp. dill

1 egg

½ c. water (add slowly)

Preheat oven to 350°. Slice lox and finely grind it in a food processor.

Combine all ingredients (except the water) together. Add water slowly and mix until a dough forms (if too dry, add more water, too wet, add a bit more flour). You may not need all the water if you reach a good consistency first. Roll out on a lightly floured surface to ¼" thickness. Use a cookie cutter (or a knife) to cut into shapes. Line a cookie sheet with parchment paper (for easy cleanup), and place the cookies on the sheet (they can be rather close together as they don't grow much while cooking).

Bake 22-27 minutes or until golden brown. Transfer and let cool completely on a wire rack. Store the cookies in an airtight container in the refrigerator. For more options, read the "Storage Tips" section on page 18.

CANINE QUICHE

{ DELECTABLE QUICHES FOR THAT
EXTRA SPECIAL PUP }

¹/₂ c. pureed carrots

¹/₂ c. tightly packed spinach leaves

¹/₂ c. lean ground pork (pre-cooked and drained)

1 ¹/₂ c. oat flour

¹/₂ c. oat bran

2 eggs

¹/₂ c. low-fat cottage cheese

1 tsp. basil

Preheat oven to 400°. Peel, dice and puree carrots in a food processor. Puree spinach leaves in a food processor until smooth. Grind the drained pork in a food processor.

Combine all ingredients together and mix thoroughly. Spray cooking spray throughly into a mini muffin pan (or a regular muffin pan). Push mixture evenly into the papers (the consistency will be similar to meatloaf) coming close to the top (the mix will not rise very much).

Bake 10-15 minutes if using the mini muffin pan or 20-25 minutes if using a regular sized muffin pan. Quiches are done when a toothpick inserted into the center comes out clean. Remove from the oven and let cool completely on a wire rack. Store in an airtight container in the refrigerator.

Note: A dollop of non-fat cream cheese or sour cream on top of these makes them an even more special treat. These are also a great option to vary the ingredients to make different flavored quiches based on your dog's favorite things. Here are a few suggesstions:

- Swap the pork for beef and the cottage cheese for Swiss cheese

- Swap the pork for bacon and the cottage cheese for cheddar cheese

- Swap the pork for turkey and the cottage cheese for Swiss cheese

The possibilities are endless...

SPINACH—LEAN & GREEN

There must be something in spinach that enables Popeye to "fight to the finish" after he eats it. What there is is a solid helping of fiber, the minerals calcium and potassium, and the vitamins A, B6, and K. Spinach also has twice the iron content of most other greens, and it is a recognized source of antioxidants. Avoid Popeye's source—canned spinach—and instead choose organically grown regular or baby spinach and feed it lightly steamed or raw (chopped up fine).

ASNACKADOPOULIS

{ TOTO, WE'RE NOT IN ATHENS ANYMORE }

1 c. tightly packed spinach leaves

1 ½ c. oat flour

1 ½ c. brown rice flour

½ c. feta cheese

1 egg

½ c. water (add slowly)

Preheat oven to 375°. Puree spinach in a food processor.

Combine all ingredients (except the water) together. Add water slowly and mix until a dough forms (if too dry, add more water, too wet, add a bit more flour). You may not need all the water if you reach a good consistency first. Roll out on a lightly floured surface to ¼" thickness. Use a cookie cutter (or a knife) to cut into shapes. Line a cookie sheet with parchment paper (for easy cleanup), and place the cookies on the sheet (they can be rather close together as they don't grow much while cooking).

Bake 22-27 minutes or until golden brown. Transfer and let cool completely on a wire rack. Store the cookies in an airtight container in the refrigerator. For more options, read the "Storage Tips" section on page 18.

THE ONLY TRUE PÂTÉ

{ WHY, IT'S LIVER OF COURSE }

2 c. oat flour

$\frac{1}{2}$ c. oat bran

$\frac{1}{2}$ c. raw chicken (or beef) livers

2 eggs

Preheat oven to 375°. Puree the liver in a food processor. Immediately clean out the food processor afterward. Liver is very hard to get out once it dries, trust us.

Combine all ingredients together and mix thoroughly. Line a 9" square pan with parchment paper (you'll thank us for this) and pour the mixture in.

Bake 35-40 minutes or until sides of seem to be loosening from the pan. Cool completely in the pan. Store the cookies in an airtight container in the refrigerator. For more options, read the "Storage Tips" section on page 18.

A THANKSGIVING PRELUDE

{ AN EARLY START FOR THE BIG DAY }

1 ½ c. oat flour

1 ½ c. brown rice flour

½ c. oat bran

½ c. sweet potato or yams (cooked and mashed, or canned)

½ c. ground turkey (cooked and drained)

1 tsp. parsley

1 tsp. sage

1 tsp. rosemary

½ c. dried cranberries

1 egg

½ c. water (add slowly)

Preheat oven to 350°. Grind the turkey in a food processor.

Combine all ingredients and mix thoroughly until a dough forms. Roll the dough into 1" balls and place on a cookie sheet lined with parchment paper (for easier cleanup). Treats can be placed close together as they don't spread while cooking.

Bake for 25-30 minutes or until golden brown. Transfer and let cool completely on a wire rack. Store the cookies in an airtight container in the refrigerator. For more options, read the "Storage Tips" section on page 18.

THATSA TASTY
MEATBALL

{ ALL IT NEEDS IS A LITTLE MARINARA }

2 lbs. raw, lean ground beef (or turkey)

$^1/_2$ c. grated parmesan cheese

$^1/_2$ c. oat bran

1 tsp. dried oregano

1 tsp. dried parsley

1 tsp. dried basil

1 egg

Preheat oven to 350°. Combine all ingredients together and mix thoroughly. Roll mixture into 1" balls and place on a cookie sheet lined with parchment paper (makes for easier cleanup). We recommend using rubber or latex gloves to form and roll the meatballs. It's a lot more pleasant that way.

Bake 15-20 minutes or until evenly browned and cooked through. Remove from the oven and let cool. Store in an airtight container in the refrigerator.

Notes: These freeze very well. We recommend placing a small amount in the refrigerator and the rest in a bag in the freezer. When you need more you have them ready and on hand.

This is a great item to alternate proteins in. You can do 1 lb. beef with 1 lb. pork to make a mixed meatball. You can also use chicken or turkey to make a poultry version of this recipe.

TAKE-OUT ROYALTY

{ THE MOST PROLIFIC COMBINATION
EVER TO BE PRINTED ON A CHINESE MENU }

1 ½ c. oat flour

1 ½ c. brown rice flour

½ c. oat bran

½ c. ground chicken (cooked)

½ c. pureed broccoli

2 tbsp. blackstrap molasses

1 egg

½ c. water (add slowly)

Preheat oven to 350°. Drain the chicken, then grind in a food processor.

Combine all ingredients (except the water) together. Add water slowly and mix until a dough forms (if too dry, add more water, too wet, add a bit more flour). You may not need all the water if you reach a good consistency first. Roll out on a lightly floured surface to ¼" thickness. Use a cookie cutter (or a knife) to cut into shapes. Line a cookie sheet with parchment paper (for easy cleanup), and place the

cookies on the sheet (they can be rather close together as they don't grow much while cooking).

Bake 22-27 minutes or until golden brown. Transfer and let cool completely on a wire rack. Store the cookies in an airtight container in the refrigerator. For more options, read the "Storage Tips" section on page 18.

BROCCOLI—IT'S HARD TO BEAT

If you're looking for a veggie that packs a wallop of cancer-fighting phytochemicals as well as a solid dose of vitamin C, beta carotene, folic acid, and calcium, then look no farther than the fresh, organic broccoli at your grocery store or farmer's market. Chop or puree it raw before adding it to your dog's meals (or treats), or lightly steam it and cut it up—using the broth created by the steam, too. Good stuff!

CHAPTER 4

THE COOKIE JAR

A little something for the sweet tooth

We all indulge ourselves with sweets, so why not our dogs? They appreciate them, too. As you'll learn from these recipes and the sidebars in this chapter, the key is to give them sweets that won't upset their digestive system and that aren't harmful (remember, never give chocolate to dogs!). With this wide selection of recipes to choose from, you have lots of options to charm your companion through his sweet tooth. And let's face it, a lot of dogs love the sweets as much as the meats. Here's to the sweet hounds!

Choose to use organic ingredients in these recipes, like we do!

THE CLASSIC

{ THE KEYSTONE TO ANY COOKIE JAR – THE DOG-SAFE VERSION OF THE CHOCOLATE CHIP COOKIE }

1 ½ c. oat flour

1 ½ c. brown rice flour

½ c. carob chips (can NOT be substituted with chocolate)

1 egg

1 tsp. vanilla

½ c. water (add slowly)

Preheat oven to 350˚. Combine all ingredients (except the water) together. Add water slowly and mix until a dough forms (if too dry, add more water, too wet, add a bit more flour). You may not need all the water if you reach a good consistency first. Roll into small balls (about 1" in diameter) and place on an ungreased cookie sheet (they can be rather close together as they don't spread while cooking). Press each one down with your hand to flatten the cookies.

Bake 22-27 minutes or until golden brown. Transfer and let cool completely on a wire rack. Store the cookies in an airtight container in the refrigerator. For more options, read the "Storage Tips" section on page 18.

CAROB

Carob pods come from carob trees, which are small evergreen shrubs native to the Mediterranean. Before the use of sugar cane, carob was used as a natural sweetener. In fact, the pods have a taste reminiscent of sweetened cocoa, but without the theobromine, caffeine, or other psychoactive properties of cocoa (which are potentially lethal for dogs). Mixed with saturated fats, carob bars and chips can be safely substituted for chocolate. It is important to remember never to give a dog chocolate.

SNICKERDOODLES

{ NOW THE DOGS HAVE THEIR OWN }

1 ½ c. oat flour

1 ½ c. brown rice flour

2 tsp. cinnamon

1 egg

¼ c. honey

1 tsp. vanilla

½ c. water (add slowly)

Preheat oven to 375°. Combine all ingredients (except the water) together. Add water slowly and mix until a dough forms (if too dry, add more water, too wet, add a bit more flour). You may not need all the water if you reach a good consistency first. Spoon out mixture and roll into balls (about 1" in diameter). Line a cookie sheet with parchment paper (for easy cleanup), and place the cookies on the sheet (they can be rather close together as they don't grow much while cooking). Using a fork, press down the balls, flattening them and adding decorative lines in the tops.

Bake 18-25 minutes or until golden brown. Transfer and let cool completely on a wire rack. Store the cookies in an airtight container in the refrigerator. For more options, read the "Storage Tips" section on page 18.

LUMBERJACK SNACKS

{ A COOL PEANUT BUTTER AND FRUIT SNACK
FOR THOSE HARD-WORKING DOGS }

1 c. rolled oats (the old-fashioned kind, not instant)

1 c. oat bran

$1/4$ c. dried cranberries

$1/4$ c. finely chopped peanuts

$1/4$ c. shredded coconut (unsweetened)

$1/4$ c. honey

$1/2$ c. peanut butter (unsalted)

Mix all ingredients together. Drop mixture by tablespoon into mini cupcake papers and place on a rimmed baking sheet or large plate. Put in the refrigerator for 15 minutes, or until set. Store the cookies in an airtight container in the refrigerator. For more options, read the "Storage Tips" section on page 18.

PUMPKIN DROPS

{ HEAVENLY PUMPKIN SPICE COOKIES }

1 $\frac{1}{2}$ c. oat flour

1 $\frac{1}{2}$ c. brown rice flour

$\frac{1}{2}$ tsp. cinnamon

$\frac{1}{2}$ tsp. ground ginger

1 egg

3 tbsp. applesauce (unsweetened)

$\frac{3}{4}$ c. canned pumpkin (or fresh, pureed pumpkin)

$\frac{1}{2}$ c. water (add slowly)

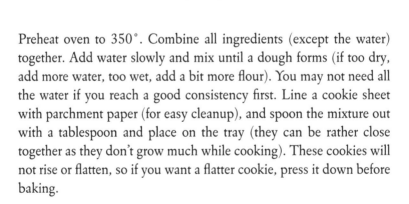

Preheat oven to 350°. Combine all ingredients (except the water) together. Add water slowly and mix until a dough forms (if too dry, add more water, too wet, add a bit more flour). You may not need all the water if you reach a good consistency first. Line a cookie sheet with parchment paper (for easy cleanup), and spoon the mixture out with a tablespoon and place on the tray (they can be rather close together as they don't grow much while cooking). These cookies will not rise or flatten, so if you want a flatter cookie, press it down before baking.

Bake 18-25 minutes or until golden brown. Transfer and let cool completely on a wire rack. Store the cookies in an airtight container in the refrigerator. For more options, read the "Storage Tips" section on page 18.

OUT OF THE PATCH, AND INTO THE BOWL

Pumpkin is a nutritious and delicious food whose benefits can be reaped by including it in recipes that go well beyond the traditional holiday pie—and your dog shouldn't be getting any of that pie, anyway! Pumpkin is high in potassium and beta carotene (a natural antioxidant) but low in calories, so when steamed and eaten in chunks or pureed, it's great for those watching their weight who want to enjoy a flavorful and filling veggie. A tablespoon or two of canned (or fresh) pumpkin added to their food will firm up your dog's stool if he has diarrhea or help loosen it if he is constipated (it's true, it works both ways). It's a miracle food!

GINGER SNAPS

{ THE GINGER SNAPS SO YOU DON'T HAVE TO }

2 c. oat flour

2 c. brown rice flour

2 tsp. baking soda

2 tsp. ground ginger

1 tsp. cinnamon

1 tsp. ground cloves

1 egg

¹/₄ c. safflower oil

¹/₂ c. molasses (blackstrap or regular)

¹/₂ c. water

Preheat oven to 375°. Combine all ingredients (except the water) together. Add water slowly and mix until a dough forms (if too dry, add more water, too wet, add a bit more flour). You may not need all the water if you reach a good consistency first. Spoon out mixture and roll into balls (about 1" in diameter). Line a cookie sheet with parchment paper (for easy cleanup), and place the cookies on the sheet (they can be rather close together as they don't grow much while cooking). These cookies will not rise or flatten, so if you want a flatter cookie, press it down before baking.

Bake 18-25 minutes or until golden brown. Transfer and let cool completely on a wire rack. Store the cookies in an airtight container in the refrigerator. For more options, read the "Storage Tips" section on page 18.

GINGER

Besides having a smell that instantly transforms a house into a home (just as a dog does), ginger is a tasty and nutritious spice. It is especially beneficial for stomach upset.

OATMEAL COOKIES

{ AS GOOD AS YOU REMEMBER }

1 ½ c. oat flour

1 ½ c. brown rice flour

1 tsp. baking powder

½ tsp. baking soda

1 c. rolled oats (old-fashioned kind, not instant)

½ c. finely chopped peanuts (unsalted)

2 eggs

¼ c. safflower oil

½ c. peanut butter (unsalted)

½ c. honey

1 tsp. vanilla

Preheat oven to 375°. Combine all ingredients (except the water) together. Add water slowly and mix until a dough forms (if too dry, add more water, too wet, add a bit more flour). You may not need all the water if you reach a good consistency first. Line a cookie sheet with parchment paper (for easy cleanup), and spoon out mixture and roll into balls (about 1" in diameter). Place on the sheet (they can be rather close together as they don't grow much while cooking). Press each one down with your hand to flatten the cookies if you want; they don't flatten while cooking.

Bake 18-25 minutes or until golden brown. Transfer and let cool completely on a wire rack. Store the cookies in an airtight container in the refrigerator. For more options, read the "Storage Tips" section on page 18.

COCONUT CREMES

{ THE FRUIT OF THE ISLANDS }

1 ½ c. oat flour

1 ½ c. brown rice flour

½ c. shredded coconut (unsweetened)

½ c. carob chips (can NOT be substituted with chocolate)

1 egg

½ c. peanut butter (unsalted)

1 tsp. vanilla

½ c. water (add slowly)

Preheat oven to 375°. Combine all ingredients (except the water) together. Add water slowly and mix until a dough forms (if too dry, add more water, too wet, add a bit more flour). You may not need all the water if you reach a good consistency first. Spoon out mixture and roll into balls (about 1" in diameter). Line a cookie sheet with parchment paper (for easy cleanup), and spoon out mixture and roll into balls (about 1" in diameter). Place on the sheet (they can be rather close together as they don't grow much while cooking).

Bake 18-25 minutes or until golden brown. Transfer and let cool completely on a wire rack. Store the cookies in an airtight container in the refrigerator. For more options, read the "Storage Tips" section on page 18.

HONEY MUTTS

{ A TASTY HONEY AND OAT COOKIE }

1 ½ c. brown rice flour

2 c. rolled oats (old-fashioned kind, not instant)

1 egg

½ c. peanut butter (unsalted)

4 tbsp. applesauce (unsweetened)

¼ c. honey

¼ c. water (add slowly)

Preheat oven to 375°. Combine all ingredients (except the water) together. Add water slowly and mix until a dough forms (if too dry, add more water, too wet, add a bit more flour). You may not need all the water if you reach a good consistency first. Line a cookie sheet with parchment paper (for easy cleanup), and spoon out mixture and roll into balls (about 1" in diameter). Place on the sheet (they can be rather close together as they don't grow much while cooking). Press each one down with your hand to flatten.

Bake 18-25 minutes or until golden brown. Transfer and let cool completely on a wire rack. Store the cookies in an airtight container in the refrigerator. For more options, read the "Storage Tips" section on page 18.

131

TRAIL MIX

{ TRAIL SNACKS FOR YOUR BEST PAL }

1 ¼ c. oat flour

1 ¼ c. brown rice flour

½ c. carob chips (can NOT be substituted for chocolate)

½ c. granola (can NOT contain raisins)

½ c. shredded coconut (unsweetened)

½ c. dried cranberries

1 egg

¼ c. molasses (blackstrap or regular)

½ c. water (add slowly)

Preheat oven to 375°. Combine all ingredients (except the water) together. Add water slowly and mix until a dough forms (if too dry, add more water, too wet, add a bit more flour). You may not need all the water if you reach a good consistency first. Line a cookie sheet with parchment paper (for easy cleanup), and spoon out mixture and roll into balls (about 1" in diameter). Place on the sheet (they can be rather close together as they don't grow much while cooking). Press each one down with your hand to flatten the cookies if you want; they don't flatten while cooking.

Bake 18-25 minutes or until golden brown. Transfer and let cool completely on a wire rack. Store the cookies in an airtight container in the refrigerator. For more options, read the "Storage Tips" section on page 18.

RID YOUR DOG'S PANTRY OF RAISINS

Though scientists haven't pinpointed what it is in raisins, especially, that's toxic to dogs, they've seen plenty of cases of acute renal failure in dogs that have eaten various amounts of raisins (and grapes) to know that they contain something quite harmful. The veterinarian community is clear that raisins and grapes should not be fed to dogs.

CRANBERRY CHUNK COOKIES

{ DIDN'T YOU SAY CHOCOLATE WAS BAD? NOT WHITE CHOCOLATE! }

1 ½ c. oat flour

1 ½ c. brown rice flour

½ c. dried cranberries

½ c. shredded coconut (unsweetened)

½ c. white chocolate chips or chunks

1 egg

½ c. water (add slowly)

Preheat oven to 375°. Combine all ingredients (except the water) together. Add water slowly and mix until a dough forms (if too dry, add more water, too wet, add a bit more flour). You may not need all the water if you reach a good consistency first. Line a cookie sheet with parchment paper (for easy cleanup), and spoon out mixture and roll into balls (about 1" in diameter). Place on the sheet (they can be rather close together as they don't grow much while cooking). Press each one down with your hand to flatten the cookies if you want; they don't flatten while cooking.

Bake 18-25 minutes or until golden brown. Transfer and let cool completely on a wire rack. Store the cookies in an airtight container in the refrigerator. For more options, read the "Storage Tips" section on page 18.

WHITE CHOCOLATE IN MODERATION

Why is white chocolate ok for dogs but milk or dark chocolate is an absolute no-no? Because white chocolate is really not chocolate at all. It is a mixture of cocoa butter, sugar, and milk. Originally made in Switzerland, it didn't become popular in the US until the 1980s. Now it is marketed alongside regular chocolates as an equally creamy and sweet confection—and in limited quantities, is a safe addition to canine cookies.

LIL' TASTE O' PIE

{ APPLE PIE—A PERENNIAL HOLIDAY FAVORITE, NOW BITE-SIZE FOR YOUR PUP }

1 ½ c. oat flour

1 ½ c. brown rice flour

2 ½ tsp. cinnamon

½ c. oat bran

1 egg

½ c. applesauce (unsweetened)

2 tbsp. honey

¼ c. water (add slowly)

Preheat oven to 375°. Combine all ingredients (except the water) together. Add water slowly and mix until a dough forms (if too dry, add more water, too wet, add a bit more flour). You may not need all the water if you reach a good consistency first. Line a cookie sheet with parchment paper (for easy cleanup), and spoon out mixture and roll into balls (about 1" in diameter). Place on the sheet (they can be rather close together as they don't grow much while cooking). Press each one down with your hand to flatten the cookies if you want; they don't flatten while cooking.

Bake 18-25 minutes or until golden brown. Transfer and let cool completely on a wire rack. Store the cookies in an airtight container in the refrigerator. For more options, read the "Storage Tips" section on page 18.

AN APPLE A DAY

You know the old saying, "An apple a day keeps the doctor away"? The same, thankfully, can be said for dogs. Apples that have been thoroughly washed, had the stems and seeds removed and cut up into slices or chunks make great healthy snacks for dogs. Apples have numerous health benefits.

BLUEBERRY BITES

{ LITTLE BITES OF BLUEBERRY GOODNESS }

1 ½ c. oat flour

1 ½ c. brown rice flour

½ c. frozen blueberries (or fresh)

1 egg

½ c. peanut butter (unsalted)

½ c. water (add slowly)

Preheat oven to 375°. Combine all ingredients (except the water) together. Add water slowly and mix until a dough forms (if too dry, add more water, too wet, add a bit more flour). You may not need all the water if you reach a good consistency first. Line a cookie sheet with parchment paper (for easy cleanup), and spoon out mixture and roll into balls (about 1" in diameter). Place on the sheet (they can be rather close together as they don't grow much while cooking). Press each one down with your hand to flatten the cookies if you want; they don't flatten while cooking.

Bake 18-25 minutes or until golden brown. Transfer and let cool completely on a wire rack. Store the cookies in an airtight container in the refrigerator. For more options, read the "Storage Tips" section on page 18.

P.B. BANANA DROPS

{ BOATLOADS OF OATS AND BANANAS }

1 ½ c. oat flour

1 ½ c. brown rice flour

½ c. peanut butter (unsalted)

½ c. rolled oats (old-fashioned kind, not instant)

1 egg

½ c. bananas (mashed & pureed)

½ c. water (add slowly)

Preheat oven to 375°. Combine all ingredients (except the water) together. Add water slowly and mix until a dough forms (if too dry, add more water, too wet, add a bit more flour). You may not need all the water if you reach a good consistency first. Line a cookie sheet with parchment paper (for easy cleanup), and spoon out mixture and roll into balls (about 1" in diameter). Place on the sheet (they can be rather close together as they don't grow much while cooking). Press each one down with your hand to flatten the cookies if you want; they don't flatten while cooking.

Bake 18-25 minutes or until golden brown. Transfer and let cool completely on a wire rack. Store the cookies in an airtight container in the refrigerator. For more options, read the "Storage Tips" section.

PEANUT CLUSTERS
{ A PEANUT BUTTER CRUNCH COOKIE }

1 ½ c. oat flour

1 ½ c. brown rice flour

½ c. finely chopped peanuts (unsalted)

½ c. shredded coconut (unsweetened)

½ c. rolled oats (old-fashioned kind, not instant)

2 eggs

¼ c. molasses (blackstrap or regular)

½ c. peanut butter

½ c. water (add slowly)

Preheat oven to 375°. Combine all ingredients (except the water) together. Add water slowly and mix until a dough forms (if too dry, add more water, too wet, add a bit more flour). You may not need all the water if you reach a good consistency first. Line a cookie sheet with parchment paper (for easy cleanup), and spoon out mixture and roll into balls (about 1" in diameter). Place on the sheet (they can be rather close together as they don't grow much while cooking). These cookies will not rise or flatten, so if you want a flatter cookie, press it down before baking.

Bake 18-25 minutes or until golden brown. Transfer and let cool completely on a wire rack. Store the cookies in an airtight container in the refrigerator. For more options, read the "Storage Tips" section on page 18.

COCONUT

Coconut is an excellent source of lauric acid, manganese, iron, phosphorus, and potassium. It is a rich protein source that supports skin and coat health. It supports healthy function of the thyroid, immune system, gastrointestinal, digestive, cell, and bone function.

MUDDY PAWS

{ THE ONLY ACCEPTABLE KIND IN THE HOUSE }

1 ½ c. oat flour

1 ½ c. brown rice flour

¼ c. carob powder (can NOT be substituted with chocolate)

½ c. carob chips (can NOT be substituted with chocolate)

1 egg

½ c. peanut butter (unsalted)

1 tbsp. honey

⅔ c. water (add slowly)

Preheat oven to 375°. Combine all ingredients (except the water) together. Add water slowly and mix until a dough forms (if too dry, add more water, too wet, add a bit more flour). You may not need all the water if you reach a good consistency first. Line a cookie sheet with parchment paper (for easy cleanup), and spoon out mixture and roll into balls (about 1" in diameter). Place on the sheet (they can be rather close together as they don't grow much while cooking). These cookies will not rise or flatten, so if you want a flatter cookie, press it down before baking.

Bake 18-25 minutes or until golden brown. Transfer and let cool completely on a wire rack. Store the cookies in an airtight container in the refrigerator. For more options, read the "Storage Tips" section on page 18.

Note: Carob powder and carob chips are generally carried in all health food stores or are available online.

PEANUT BUTTER

As oily as it looks, peanut butter is high in monounsaturated fats—the kind that protect against heart disease. Grinding your own (organic) nuts yields a butter of exceptional flavor and avoids the sugars and salts that are often added to commercial varieties. Peanuts are an excellent source of protein, as well.

SNOWBALLS

{ COCONUT-COVERED BALLS OF GOODNESS }

1 ½ c. oat flour

1 ½ c. brown rice flour

1 c. shredded coconut (unsweetened)

1 tsp. cinnamon

1 egg

1 tsp. vanilla

½ c. coconut milk (add slowly)

Preheat oven to 375°. Combine all ingredients (except the coconut and coconut water) together. Add coconut water slowly and mix until a dough forms (if too dry, add more water, too wet, add a bit more flour). You may not need all the water if you reach a good consistency first. Line a cookie sheet with parchment paper (for easy cleanup). Spoon out mixture and roll into balls (about 1" in diameter) in the coconut. Place the cookies on the sheet (they can be rather close together as they don't grow much while cooking).

Bake 18-25 minutes or until golden brown. Transfer and let cool completely on a wire rack. Store the cookies in an airtight container in the refrigerator. For more options, read the "Storage Tips" section on page 18.

GOING NUTS

{ THAT'S GOING TO BE YOUR DOG'S REACTION }

1 1/2 c. oat flour

1 1/2 c. brown rice flour

1/2 c. finely ground peanuts

1 egg

1/2 c. molasses (blackstap or regular)

1 tsp. vanilla

1/2 c. water (add slowly)

Preheat oven to 375°. Combine all ingredients (except the water) together. Add water slowly and mix until a dough forms (if too dry, add more water, too wet, add a bit more flour). You may not need all the water if you reach a good consistency first. Line a cookie sheet with parchment paper (for easy cleanup), and spoon out mixture and roll into balls (about 1" in diameter). Place on the sheet (they can be rather close together as they don't grow much while cooking). These cookies will not rise or flatten, so if you want a flatter cookie, press it down before baking.

Bake 18-25 minutes or until golden brown. Transfer and let cool completely on a wire rack. Store the cookies in an airtight container in the refrigerator. For more options, read the "Storage Tips" section on page 18.

PUPPERMINTS

{ THESE ARE SURE TO STRAIGHTEN THEIR TAIL – AND FRESHEN THEIR BREATH }

1 ½ c. oat flour

1 ½ c. brown rice flour

½ c. dried mint

¼ tsp. peppermint oil

1 egg

½ c. water (add slowly)

Preheat oven to 375˚. Combine all ingredients (except the water) together. Add water slowly and mix until a dough forms (if too dry, add more water, too wet, add a bit more flour). You may not need all the water if you reach a good consistency first. Line a cookie sheet with parchment paper (for easy cleanup), and spoon out mixture and roll into balls (about 1" in diameter). Place on the sheet (they can be rather close together as they don't grow much while cooking). These cookies will not rise or flatten, so if you want a flatter cookie, press it down before baking.

Bake 18-25 minutes or until golden brown. Transfer and let cool completely on a wire rack. Store the cookies in an airtight container in the refrigerator. For more options, read the "Storage Tips" section on page 18.

PEPPERMINT

Mints have long been associated with aiding in digestive upset, and this is true for dogs as well as people. They have the added benefit of being able to freshen breath. A double-whammy for dogs!

GINGERBREAD SNACKS

{ A SEASONAL FAVORITE FOR EVERYONE }

1 ½ c. oat flour

1 ½ c. brown rice flour

1 tsp. baking powder

1 tsp. ground ginger

1 tsp. cinnamon

½ tsp. baking soda

1 egg

¼ c. safflower oil

½ c. molasses (blackstrap or regular)

¼ c. peanut butter (unsalted)

1 tbsp. apple cider vinegar

½ c. water (add slowly)

Preheat oven to 375°. Combine all ingredients (except the water) together. Add water slowly and mix until a dough forms (if too dry, add more water, too wet, add a bit more flour). You may not need all the water if you reach a good consistency first. Line a cookie sheet with parchment paper (for easy cleanup), and spoon out mixture and roll into balls (about 1" in diameter). Place on the sheet (they can be rather close together as they don't grow much while cooking). These cookies will not rise or flatten, so if you want a flatter cookie, press it down before baking.

Bake 18-25 minutes or until golden brown. Transfer and let cool completely on a wire rack. Store the cookies in an airtight container in the refrigerator. For more options, read the "Storage Tips" section on page 18.

APPLE CIDER VINEGAR

It seems you can't go wrong giving your dog apple cider vinegar—inside and out! The easiest way to introduce it to your dog's regular diet is to put a tiny amount in the water bowl. As he becomes used to the taste, increase the amount ever so gradually until you are adding about a teaspoon a day in the water. ACV is good for arthritis, allergies, itchy skin, correcting pH levels, eliminating tear stains around the eyes, fighting fleas and other pests, and so much more!

STRAWBERRY-BANANA COOKIES

{ WHAT A WINNING PAIR THESE TWO ARE }

....

1 $\frac{1}{2}$ c. oat flour

1 $\frac{1}{2}$ c. brown rice flour

1 tsp. cinnamon

1 tsp. honey

1 egg

$\frac{1}{2}$ c. strawberries (fresh or frozen, mashed and pureed)

$\frac{1}{2}$ c. bananas (mashed and pureed)

$\frac{1}{2}$ c. water (add slowly)

Preheat oven to 375°. Combine all ingredients (except the water) together. Add water slowly and mix until a dough forms (if too dry, add more water, too wet, add a bit more flour). You may not need all the water if you reach a good consistency first.

Line a cookie sheet with parchment paper (for easy cleanup), and spoon out mixture and roll into balls (about 1" in diameter). Place on the sheet (they can be rather close together as they don't grow much while cooking). These cookies will not rise or flatten, so if you want a flatter cookie, press it down before baking.

Bake 18-25 minutes or until golden brown. Transfer and let cool completely on a wire rack. Store the cookies in an airtight container in the refrigerator. For more options, read the "Storage Tips" section on page 18.

CHAPTER 5

5th AVE.
DECADENCE

For those with richer tastes

This collection of sweets strays from the path of the others by exploring combinations that are both indulgent and delightful. Some are simple, some are sinful. Like a stroll down Manhattan's 5th Avenue, where the riches of the world entice you, these goodies will have your dog pining by the cookie jar. This is also where you'll find recipes for cakes, cupcakes and muffins as well as icing options.

BANANA NUT BISCOTTYS

{ STRAIGHT FROM THE MOST UPSCALE CAFE }

$^1/_2$ c. bananas

2 $^1/_2$ c. oat flour

2 $^1/_2$ c. brown rice flour

2 tsp. baking powder

$^1/_2$ tsp baking soda

2 eggs

1 tsp. vanilla

1 tbsp. honey

$^1/_4$ c. finely chopped peanuts

A small container of water

Preheat oven to 325°. Mash bananas and puree in a food processor.

Combine all ingredients together in a food processor (or by hand in a bowl). Add 1 tbsp. of water at a time until the dough reaches a workable consistency. Once the dough is formed, knead together by hand for several minutes on a lightly floured surface. Separate into two logs about 12" long by 4" wide and 1" high. Line a cookie sheet with parchment paper (for easy cleanup), and place the biscottys on the sheet (they can be rather close together as they don't grow much while cooking).

Bake for 30 minutes. Remove and let cool on the baking sheet for 10 minutes. Slice pieces ½" thick. Bake an additional 20 minutes. Remove and place on a wire rack to cool completely. Store the cookies in an airtight container in the refrigerator. For more options, read the "Storage Tips" section on page 18.

CRANBERRY SCONES

{ A PERFECT TEA-TIME TREAT }

1 ½ c. oat flour

1 ½ c. brown rice flour

2 tsp. baking powder

½ c. peanut butter (unsalted)

¼ c. safflower oil

1 egg

½ c. water (add slowly)

½ c. dried cranberries

Preheat oven to 400°. Set cranberries aside for later. Combine all ingredients (except the water) together. Add water slowly and mix until a dough forms (if too dry, add more water, too wet, add a bit more flour). You may not need all the water if you reach a good consistency first. Once combined, gently stir in cranberries by hand. Line a cookie sheet with parchment paper (for easy cleanup), and scoop out heaping spoonfuls (they can be rather close together as they don't grow much while cooking).

Bake 15-20 minutes or until a toothpick inserted into the center of the scone comes out cleanly. Remove from the oven and let cool completely. Store the cookies in an airtight container in the refrigerator. For more options, read the "Storage Tips" section on page 18.

BERRY, BERRY YUMMY

Several of the recipes in this chapter call for various berries, including cranberries, blueberries, and strawberries. Wonder no longer, all are safe for dogs. Berries are natural antioxidants; in fact, recent studies have shown that blueberries are especially rich in them. Cranberries are known for relieving urinary tract infections and promoting uterine health. Berries also contain lots of vitamin C. They are naturally sweet and tasty, and dogs really enjoy them. They can be served fresh, frozen, or dried.

SWEET POTATO PIES

{ IT'S EXACTLY WHAT YOU THINK, BUT SMALLER }

FOR DOUGH:

1 c. oat flour

$\frac{1}{2}$ c. brown rice flour

$\frac{1}{4}$ c. safflower oil

$\frac{1}{4}$ c. water

1 egg

FOR FILLING:

1 c. cooked, mashed sweet potato (or pumpkin)

1 tsp. cinnamon

1 tbsp. honey

1 tsp. ground cloves

1 egg

Preheat oven to 400°. Combine all ingredients (except the water) together. Add water slowly and mix until a dough forms (if too dry, add more water, too wet, add a bit more flour). You may not need all the water if you reach a good consistency first. Roll out on a lightly floured surface to $1/4$" thickness. Use a 2" circle cookie cutter (or top of a glass, if you don't have a circle cookie cutter) to cut into shapes. Thoroughly spray cooking spray into the cups of a lightly greased mini muffin pan and press each circle down into the cups.

Combine all the filling ingredients together and mix thoroughly. Scoop even amounts into each of the crusts in the muffin pan.

Bake for 15-20 minutes or until the edges of the crust are golden brown. Store the cookies in an airtight container in the refrigerator. For more options, read the "Storage Tips" section on page 18.

APPLE SPICE MUFFINS

**{ A TASTY LITTLE TREAT THAT SMELLS SO GOOD
YOU'LL WANT THEM FOR YOURSELF }**

1 ½ c. oat flour

1 ½ c. brown rice flour

1 tbsp. baking powder

1 tsp. cinnamon

2 eggs

¾ c. honey

1 c. applesauce (unsweetened)

¼ c. safflower oil

Preheat oven to 350°. Combine all ingredients together and mix thoroughly. Place cupcake papers into a muffin pan. Spoon mixture evenly into the papers close to the top.

Bake 18-22 minutes or until a toothpick inserted into the center comes out clean. Remove from the oven and let cool completely on a wire rack. Store in an airtight container in the refrigerator. For more options, read the "Storage Tips" section.

BERRY OAT BITES

{ A CHEWY TREAT THAT LIVES UP TO ITS NAME }

1 ½ c. oat flour

1 c. rolled oats (old-fashioned kind, not instant)

¼ tsp. baking soda

⅔ c. honey

¼ c. safflower oil

2 ½ c. blueberries (fresh or frozen)

Preheat oven to 350°. Combine all ingredients (except blueberries) together and mix thoroughly. Separate the mixture in half. Lightly grease a muffin pan with cooking spray and press half of the mixture into the bottom of the muffin cups. Evenly spread the berries on top. Then sprinkle the remaining crumb mixture on top of the berries.

Bake for 30-35 minutes or until top is golden brown. Remove from the oven and let cool completely on a wire rack. Store in an airtight container in the refrigerator.

CAROB BROWNIES

{ THE PERFECT BROWNIE }

....

FOR BROWNIES:

2 c. oat flour

1 tsp. baking powder

5 tbsp. carob powder (can NOT be substituted with chocolate)

2 eggs

¾ c. honey

¼ c. safflower oil

½ c. non-fat vanilla yogurt (or use non-fat plain yogurt & add 1 tsp. vanilla)

——>>>•<<<——

FOR FROSTING:

8-oz. package low-fat cream cheese (at room temperature)

¼ c. carob powder

——>>>•<<<——

162

Preheat oven to 350°. Combine all brownie ingredients together. Lightly grease a 9" square pan and pour mixture in.

Bake 30-35 minutes or until sides of brownies seem to be loosening from the pan. Cool completely in the pan.

In a separate bowl, mix together frosting ingredients. Spread frosting on top of cooled brownies. Slice into the individual sized portions. Store in an airtight container in the refrigerator.

YOGURT? YOU BET!

Yogurt is another beneficial food that has been around forever. It is an excellent source of protein; because it has less milk sugar, it is easily digested, even by lactose-intolerant animals; it contains beneficial bacteria that support the digestive and immune systems; and it is a great source of calcium. A tablespoon or so of organic, plain, low-fat yogurt can benefit your dog in many ways; it is especially helpful when your dog is on antibiotics, as it restores some of the beneficial bacteria that the antibiotics randomly strip away or break down.

BANANA PUMPKIN BARS

{ TASTY BARS CHOCK-FULL OF GOODNESS }

2 c. bananas

2 c. pumpkin (canned or fresh)

1 ½ c. oat flour

1 ½ c. brown rice flour

1 c. rolled oats (old-fashioned kind, not instant)

1 tsp. cinnamon

2 eggs

¼ c. safflower oil

½ c. molasses (blackstrap or regular)

Preheat oven to 350°. Mash and puree the bananas and pumpkin, if necessary.

Combine all ingredients together until thoroughly mixed. Lightly grease a 9" square baking pan. Pour mixture into it.

Bake 30-35 minutes or until top appears golden brown and sides begin to slightly loosen from the pan. Remove from the oven and let cool completely on a wire rack. Once cool, slice into individual-sized squares. Store in an airtight container in the refrigerator.

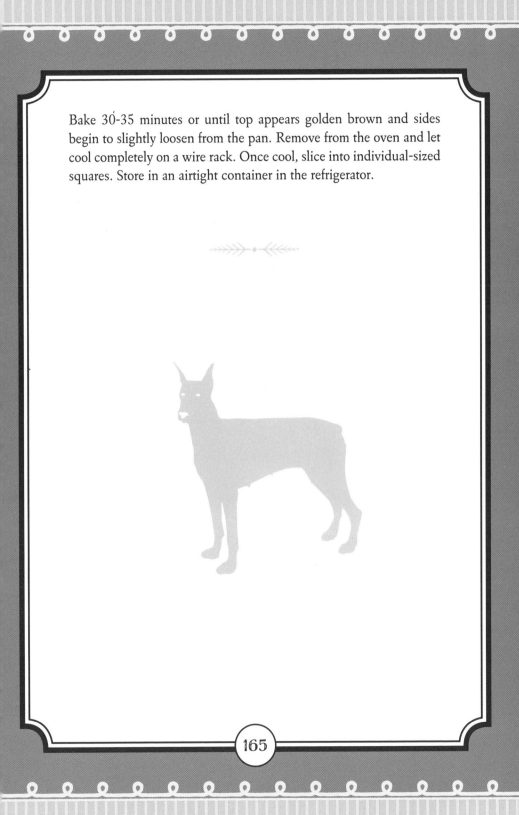

BIRTHDAY CAKE

{ CELEBRATE THAT SPECIAL DAY WITH CAKE }

FOR CAKE:

2 c. oat flour

½ c. carob powder (can NOT be substituted with chocolate)

1 tsp. baking powder

2 eggs

¼ c. safflower oil

½ c. honey

1 c. non-fat vanilla yogurt (or use non-fat plain yogurt & add 1 tsp. vanilla)

———————» • «———————

FOR ICING:

8-oz. package non-fat cream cheese (at room temperature)

1 tbsp. honey

———————» • «———————

Preheat oven to 350˚. Combine all cake ingredients together and mix thoroughly. Lightly grease a 6" round cake pan (preferably a 3" tall pan, but 2" is fine, too) and pour mixture into pan.

Bake 30-35 minutes or until a toothpick inserted in the center of the cake comes out clean. Remove from the oven and let cool completely on a wire rack.

In a separate bowl, combine icing ingredients. Once the cake is completely cooled, decorate with the icing. Store in an airtight container in the refrigerator.

BLONDIES

{ ... THEN IT'S GOT TO BE A BLONDIE! }

2 c. oat flour

1 tsp. baking powder

2 eggs

$\frac{1}{2}$ c. honey

$\frac{1}{4}$ c. peanut butter (unsalted)

$\frac{1}{4}$ c. safflower oil

$\frac{1}{2}$ c. plain or vanilla non-fat yogurt

1 c. carob chips (can NOT be substituted with chocolate)

Preheat oven to 350°. Combine flour, baking powder, eggs, honey, peanut butter, oil, and yogurt together in a large bowl. Stir in carob chips by hand until evenly mixed. Lightly grease a square 9" baking pan and pour mixture into the pan.

Bake 30-35 minutes or until the sides loosen from the pan and the top appears golden brown. Remove from the oven and let cool completely on a wire rack. Once cool, slice into individual-sized portions. Store in an airtight container in the refrigerator. For more options, read the "Storage Tips" section on page 18.

HARD ICING

{ GREAT FOR COOKIES AND GIFT GIVING }

....

This will set and be a hard icing so you can box up the treats and give them to friends and family. You can use this on top of any of the treats in this book.

FOR CAROB ICING (DARK BROWN):

1 c. unsweetened carob chips (do NOT substitute with chocolate)

FOR WHITE OR COLORED ICING:

2 c. yogurt coating chips

Natural liquid food colorings

These chips need to be heated in a double boiler (over low heat) on the oven or in the microwave. Once soft, you can either dip your treats into them, or if you're feeling ambitious, use a pastry bag with a decorating tip to ice the tops of the cookies. If the carob or yogurt chips ar too thick to work with when melted, you can add a splash of safflower oil to help thin it out, but be careful because if you add too much it won't harden again when it cools.

Carob chips, natural food colorings, and yogurt chips should be available in any health food store or the natural aisle in your local supermarket. If you are having trouble finding them, there are some great places to order them online; one site is www.barryfarm.com

BLUEBERRY MUFFINS

{ A FAVORITE TREAT FOR ALL! }

2 c. oat flour

2 tsp. baking powder

1 tsp. cinnamon

1 tsp. baking soda

2 c. blueberries (fresh or frozen)

3 eggs

$\frac{1}{4}$ c. honey

$\frac{1}{4}$ c. safflower oil

Preheat oven to 350°. Combine all ingredients together and mix thoroughly. Place cupcake papers into a mini muffin pan (or a regular muffin pan). Spoon mixture evenly into the papers almost to the top (the mix will not rise very much).

Bake 10-15 minutes if using the mini muffin pan or 22-27 minutes if using a regular-sized muffin pan. Muffins are done when a toothpick inserted into the center comes out clean. Remove from the oven and let cool completely on a wire rack. Store in an airtight container in the refrigerator. For more options, read the "Storage Tips" section.

SOFT ICING

{ CAN BE USED ON ANY TREAT }

This will be soft and require refrigeration but is a more natural "icing" if you do not want to use the carob and yogurt chips. You can use this on top of any of the treats in this book.

8-oz. package of non-fat cream cheese

2 tbsp. honey

Natural liquid food colorings

Let the cream cheese warm to room temperature and then mix the cream cheese and honey in a bowl. If you want to add color, put in a few drops of a natural food coloring at this time. Spread the icing over your cookies and store in a covered container in the refrigerator. You can find natural liquid food coloring in most health food stores.

FROZEN YOGURT SMOOTHIES

{ ICY TREATS TO BE ENJOYED ALL YEAR }

BANANA, STRAWBERRY, APPLE:

2 c. apple juice

1 mashed & pureed banana

1 c. plain non-fat yogurt

1 c. pureed strawberries

BLUEBERRY HONEY:

2 c. non-fat plain yogurt

1 c. pureed blueberries (fresh or frozen)

2 tbsp. honey

SAVORY CHICKEN CRANBERRY:

2 c. non-fat plain yogurt

2 c. chicken broth

1 c. pureed cranberries (fresh or dried)

1 tsp. rosemary

PEANUT BUTTER BACON:

2 c. plain non-fat yogurt

1 c. peanut butter (unsalted)

2 slices of bacon (cooked, drained and finely ground)

PUMPKIN PIE:

2 c. non-fat plain yogurt

1 c. canned pumpkin (fresh is always fine too)

1 tsp. cinnamon

2 tbsp. honey

CAROB CHIP CRUNCH:

2 c. non-fat plain yogurt

1 c. carob chips (can NOT be substituted for chocolate)

2 tbsp. peanut butter (unsalted)

2 tbsp. honey

———≫———•———≪———

Combine all ingredients (from respective recipe) together and whisk thoroughly. Pour mixture into an ice cube tray. Freeze until solid (at least 4 hours).

BANANA NUT PUPCAKES

{ KEEP THAT FIGURE LEAN AND MEAN! }

FOR CUPCAKES:

2 c. oat flour

2 tsp. baking powder

1/2 tsp. baking soda

1 tsp. cinnamon

1/2 c. finely chopped peanuts

3 eggs

1/4 c. honey

3 bananas

1/4 c. safflower oil

FOR ICING (OPTIONAL):

1 c. banana, mashed & pureed

8-oz. package non-fat cream cheese (at room temperature)

1 tsp. vanilla

Preheat oven to 350°. Peel, mash, and puree the bananas (for the cupcakes).

Combine all cupcake ingredients together in a large bowl. Place cupcake papers in a mini muffin pan and spoon the mixture into the cups evenly. Fill almost to the top of the papers as the cupcakes don't rise very much.

Bake 12-15 minutes or until a toothpick inserted in the center of a cupcake comes out clean. Remove from the oven and let cool completely on a wire rack.

In a separate bowl, combine icing ingredients together and mix thoroughly. Decorate the mini cupcakes. Store in an airtight container in the refrigerator.

ZUCCHINI BREAD

{ DOGS ENJOY THEIR VERSION OF THIS TREAT AS MUCH AS PEOPLE DO }

2 c. zucchini

2 c. oat flour

2 tsp. baking powder

$^1/_2$ tsp. baking soda

1 tsp. cinnamon

3 eggs

1 tsp. vanilla

$^3/_4$ c. honey

$^1/_4$ c. safflower oil

$^1/_2$ c. finely chopped peanuts (optional)

Preheat oven to 325˚. Cook, peel, slice, and puree zucchini in a food processor.

Combine all ingredients together and mix thoroughly. Lightly grease a mini loaf pan (or use a regular muffin pan with cupcake papers placed in it). Spoon mixture evenly into the pan close to the top (the mix will not rise very much).

Bake 20-25 minutes (with either pan). Bread is done when a toothpick inserted into the center comes out clean. Remove from the oven and let cool completely on a wire rack. Store in an airtight container in the refrigerator.

ZUCCHINI'S SO GOOD

Zucchini is one of several squashes that were a mainstay of Native American diets for centuries. These large, green vegetables are loaded with folate and potassium. Their peels are rich in beta-carotene and should always be included in any recipe featuring this versatile squash.

PEANUT BRITTLE

{ DOGS WILL BE BEGGING FOR MORE! }

3 c. brown rice flour

1 tsp. cinnamon

1 egg

$^{1}/_{2}$ c. honey

$^{1}/_{4}$ c. molasses (blackstrap or regular)

$^{1}/_{2}$ c. peanut butter (unsalted)

$^{1}/_{4}$ c. safflower oil

1 c. finely chopped peanuts (unsalted)

Preheat oven to 325°. Combine flour, cinnamon, egg, honey, molasses, peanut butter, and safflower oil in a food processor until completely mixed. It should form a stiff dough. Lightly grease a jelly roll pan and press the dough into the pan. Place plastic wrap or parchment paper over the pan and smooth down the mixture to $^{1}/_{4}$" thick. Remove and discard wrap or paper.

Press the chopped peanuts into the mixture. Use a knife to score the dough into individual-sized portions.

Bake 30-40 minutes or until the edges are golden brown. Cool completely in the pan on a wire rack. Once cool, break apart using the scored lines. Store in a loosely covered container at room temperature. For more options, read the "Storage Tips" section on page 18.

PUP TARTS

{ NO TOASTER NEEDED FOR THESE SNACKS! }

FOR DOUGH:

1 c. oat flour

$\frac{1}{2}$ c. brown rice flour

1 egg

$\frac{1}{4}$ c. safflower oil

$\frac{1}{4}$ c. water

FOR FILLING:

$\frac{1}{2}$ c. blueberries (fresh or frozen)

$\frac{1}{2}$ c. diced strawberries (fresh or frozen)

1 tsp. vanilla

$\frac{1}{2}$ c. peanut butter (unsalted)

1 egg

Preheat oven to 400°. Combine all dough ingredients (except the water) together. Add water slowly and mix until a dough forms (if too dry, add more water, too wet, add a bit more flour). You may not need all the water if you reach a good consistency first. Roll out on a lightly floured surface to $\frac{1}{4}$" thickness. Use a 2" circle cookie cutter (or top of a glass, if you don't have a circle cookie cutter) to cut into shapes. Thoroughly spray cooking spray into the cups of a lightly greased mini muffin pan and press each circle down into the cups.

Combine all the filling ingredients together and mix thoroughly. Scoop even amounts into each of the crusts in the muffin pan.

Bake for 15-20 minutes or until the edges of the crust are golden brown. Store the cookies in an airtight container in the refrigerator. For more options, read the "Storage Tips" section on page 18.

CAROB PUPCAKES

{ THE DOG-SAFE VERSION OF A CHOCOLATE CUPCAKE, AND PUPS LOVE THEM }

1 c. oat flour

1 c. brown rice flour

2 tsp. baking soda

$\frac{1}{2}$ tsp. baking powder

$\frac{1}{4}$ c. carob powder (can NOT be substituted with chocolate)

1 egg

2 tbsp. honey

$\frac{1}{4}$ c. water

$\frac{1}{4}$ c. safflower oil

$\frac{1}{2}$ c. plain non-fat yogurt

Preheat oven to 350°. Combine all ingredients together and mix thoroughly. Place cupcake papers into a mini muffin pan (or a regular muffin pan). Spoon mixture evenly into the papers close to the top of the papers (the mix will not rise very much).

Bake 10-15 minutes if using the mini muffin pan or 20-25 minutes if using a regular-sized muffin pan. Cupcakes are done when a toothpick inserted into the center comes out clean. Remove from the oven and let cool completely on a wire rack. Store in an airtight container in the refrigerator.

Note: These can be iced with one of the icing recipes described in earlier recipes. We recommend the soft icing recipe on page 171, and if you're feeling extra adventurous, you can add toppings to the top of the icing. Some good ideas would be ground peanuts, carob chips, granola, or sliced bananas, etc. The possibilities are endless.

TRAIL CHASERS

{ TRAIL MIX WITHOUT THE BAG }

2 c. oat flour

1 tsp. baking powder

½ c. peanut butter (unsalted)

½ c. rolled oats (old-fashioned kind, not instant)

½ c. finely chopped peanuts (unsalted)

½ c. shredded coconut (unsweetened)

½ c. dried cranberries

½ c. carob chips (can NOT be substituted with chocolate)

2 eggs

½ c. honey

1 tsp. vanilla

1 c. water

¼ c. safflower oil

Preheat oven to 350°. Combine all ingredients together and mix thoroughly. Lightly grease a 9" square baking pan and pour mixture into it.

Bake for 30-35 minutes or until top is golden brown. Remove from the oven and let cool completely on a wire rack. Once cool, slice into individual-sized portions. Store in an airtight container in the refrigerator. For more options, read the "Storage Tips" section on page 18.

A TASTE OF THE TROPICS

The Coconut Research Center in Colorado has this to say about the benefits of coconut: "Coconut is highly nutritious and rich in fiber, vitamins, and minerals. It is classified as a 'functional food' because it provides many health benefits beyond its nutritional content. Coconut oil is of special interest because it possesses healing properties far beyond that of any other dietary oil and is extensively used in traditional medicine among Asian and Pacific populations. Pacific Islanders consider coconut oil to be the cure for all illness. The coconut palm is so highly valued by them as both a source of food and medicine that it is called 'The Tree of Life.' Only recently has modern medical science unlocked the secrets to coconut's amazing healing powers." Use unsweetened coconut for dogs, but consider feeding it more often!

PUMPKIN MUFFINS

{ DOGS LOVE THE TASTE OF PUMPKIN, AND IT HELPS THEIR DIGESTIVE SYSTEM, TOO }

2 c. oat flour

2 tsp. baking powder

2 tsp. cinnamon

$\frac{1}{2}$ tsp. baking soda

$\frac{1}{2}$ tsp. ground cloves

3 eggs

$\frac{3}{4}$ c. honey

$\frac{1}{4}$ c. safflower oil

15-oz. can pumpkin (or fresh pureed pumpkin)

Preheat oven to 350°. Combine all ingredients together and mix thoroughly. Place cupcake papers into a mini muffin pan (or a regular muffin pan). Spoon mixture evenly into the papers close to the top of the papers (the mix will not rise very much).

Bake 10-15 minutes if using the mini muffin pan or 22-27 minutes if using a regular-sized muffin pan. Muffins are done when a toothpick inserted into the center comes out clean. Remove from the oven and let cool completely on a wire rack. Store in an airtight container in the refrigerator.

Note: Throwing a party for your dog with all their friends in attendance and want to make a larger cake? This is a great recipe for that, along with our other soft muffin recipes. Instead of using a cupcake pan, just pour the batter into a 6" cake pan (if you have any leftover, why not make a few muffins out of it). Keep in mind that the cake will take a lot longer to cook, so you can anticipate more like 35-40 minutes for it to finish cooking. The cake will be done when a toothpick inserted into the center comes out clean.

THE ELVIS PUPSLEYS

{ PEANUT BUTTER AND BANANA, BABY! }

1 c. bananas

2 c. oat flour

1 tsp. baking powder

$\frac{1}{2}$ tsp. baking soda

$\frac{3}{4}$ c. carob chips (can NOT be substituted for chocolate)

2 eggs

1 c. peanut butter

1 tsp. vanilla

1 tbsp. honey

$\frac{1}{4}$ c. safflower oil

Preheat oven to 350°. Peel, mash, and puree bananas in a food processor.

Combine all ingredients together and mix thoroughly. Place cupcake papers into a mini muffin pan. Spoon mixture evenly into the papers close to the top of the papers (the mix will not rise very much).

Bake 10-15 minutes or until a toothpick inserted into the center comes out clean. Remove from the oven and let cool completely on a wire rack. Store in an airtight container in the refrigerator.

Note: These can be iced with one of the icing recipes described earlier, but the King wouldn't have them any other way. And we are pretty sure that the King also would have wanted toppings on his pupsleys, so here are a few recommendations:

- *Banana slices*

- *Bacon crumbles*

- *Ground peanuts*

- *Strawberry*

Use your imagination, just stay clear of the toxic items for dogs.

CHEESECAKE BROWNIES

{ TWO GREAT TASTES THAT
TASTE GREAT TOGETHER }

2 c. oat flour

1 tsp. baking powder

5 tbsp. carob powder (can NOT be substituted with chocolate)

1 c. carob chips (can NOT be substituted with chocolate)

2 eggs

8-oz. package non-fat cream cheese

1/4 c. honey

1 tsp. vanilla

1/4 c. safflower oil

Preheat oven to 325°. Combine all ingredients together and mix thoroughly. Lightly grease a 9" square baking pan and pour mixture into it.

Bake for 30-35 minutes or until sides loosen from the pan slightly. Remove from the oven and let cool completely on a wire rack. Once cool, slice into individual-sized portions. Store in an airtight container in the refrigerator.

Note: These can be iced with one of the icing recipes described earlier.

{ CHAPTER 6 }

because you have
UNIQUE
TASTES

Special treats that meet your needs

Wouldn't it be nice if we could all eat exactly what we wanted any time we wanted it? Our bodies, however, aren't built to take that kind of abuse—and neither are those of our dogs. Add to that individual problems like allergies, sensitive stomachs, and so on, and it can sometimes seem like finding anything for them to eat is a chore. This collection of treats is designed to soothe (the bodily irritations of) the savage beast, while providing flavor and variety. At last!

Choose to use organic ingredients in these recipes, like we do!

VEGGIES ALL THE WAY

{ A CORNUCOPIA OF EARTHLY DELIGHTS }

1 ½ c. carrots

½ c. broccoli

½ c. tightly packed spinach leaves

½ c. oat flour

1 ½ c. brown rice flour

½ c. rolled oats (old-fashioned kind, not instant)

½ c. hulled sunflower seeds (unsalted)

1 egg

¼ c. water (add slowly)

THESE TREATS ARE HIGH IN FIBER,
LOW IN FAT, MEAT-FREE,
AND LOW IN PROTEIN.

Preheat oven to 350°. Peel, dice, and finely grind carrots in a food processor. Cook, dice, and finely grind broccoli in a food processor. Puree spinach in the food processor.

Combine all ingredients (except the water) together. Add water slowly and mix until a dough forms (if too dry, add more water, too wet, add a bit more flour). You may not need all the water if you reach a good consistency first. Line a cookie sheet with parchment paper (for easy cleanup), and spoon out mixture with a tablespoon and drop onto sheet (they can be rather close together as they don't grow much while cooking). These cookies will not rise or flatten, so if you want a flatter cookie, press it down before baking.

Bake 22-27 minutes or until golden brown. Transfer and let cool completely on a wire rack. Store the cookies in an airtight container in the refrigerator. For more options, read the "Storage Tips" section on page 18.

CARROTS FOR BREAKFAST...

And lunch, and dinner. Organic carrots are a wonderful regular addition to your dog's diet. They're naturally sweet, crunchy, and nutritious. Many feed their dogs carrot sticks as snacks—and dogs love them! Carrots are an exceptional source of vitamins A and C, as well as potassium. They are also high in fiber. Carrots supply nutrients necessary for the health of the eyes, immune, and digestive systems.

SPINACH POWER PUNCH

{ ALL I NEEDS IS ME SPINACH }

3 c. garbanzo bean flour (also known as chickpea flour)

¼ c. grated parmesan cheese

1 c. tightly packed spinach leaves

1 egg

½ c. water (add slowly)

>>> • <<<

THESE TREATS ARE HIGH IN FIBER, GRAIN-FREE AND MEAT-FREE.

Preheat oven to 350˚. Puree spinach leaves in a food processor until smooth.

Combine all ingredients (except the water) together. Add water slowly and mix until a dough forms (if too dry, add more water, too wet, add a bit more flour). You may not need all the water if you reach a good consistency first. Line a cookie sheet with parchment paper (for easy cleanup), and spoon out mixture with a tablespoon and drop onto sheet (they can be rather close together as they don't grow much while cooking). These cookies will not rise or flatten, so if you want a flatter cookie, press it down before baking.

Bake 22-27 minutes or until golden brown. Transfer and let cool completely on a wire rack. Store the cookies in an airtight container in the refrigerator. For more options, read the "Storage Tips" section on page 18.

SPINACH

These treats pack a one-two punch in terms of nutrition and taste. The ingredient combo in these treats is one of the best out there: whole grains, spinach, egg, and cheese. That's energy to burn, and energy to spare. And no shortage of flavor! You may find yourself snacking on these, too!

PUMPKIN PLEASERS

{ GREAT FOR THOSE WITH SENSITIVE TUMMIES }

3 c. garbanzo bean flour (also known as chickpea flour)

$^1/_2$ c. canned pumpkin (or fresh pureed pumpkin)

1 tsp. cinnamon

1 egg

$^1/_3$ c. water (add slowly)

>>> • <<<

THESE TREATS ARE HIGH IN FIBER, LOW-FAT, GRAIN-FREE, MEAT-FREE, LOW-PROTEIN & GREAT FOR SENSITIVE TUMMIES.

Preheat oven to 350°. Combine all ingredients (except the water) together. Add water slowly and mix until a dough forms (if too dry, add more water, too wet, add a bit more flour). You may not need all the water if you reach a good consistency first. Line a cookie sheet with parchment paper (for easy cleanup), and spoon out mixture with a tablespoon and drop onto sheet (they can be rather close together as they don't grow much while cooking). These cookies will not rise or flatten, so if you want a flatter cookie, press it down before baking.

Bake 22-27 minutes or until golden brown. Transfer and let cool completely on a wire rack. Store the cookie in an airtight container in the refrigerator. For more options, read the "Storage Tips" section on page 18.

PUMPKIN & YAMS

No, these won't jump out of the cookie jar and fly away, but you will find that your dog so loves them that you will fly through a batch. Like pumpkins, yams are full of potassium, fiber, beta-carotene, vitamins and minerals. Mixed with oats and honey, they turn into little "sweet potato pies"—irresistible!

SALMON SOLO

{ GRAIN-FREE FISH TREAT PERFECT FOR DOGS THAT SUFFER WITH A LOT OF ALLERGIES }

3 c. tapioca flour (or garbanzo bean flour, or amaranth flour)

2 6-oz. cans of wild salmon

1 tsp. dried rosemary

1 tsp. dried parsley

1 tsp. dried oregano

1 tsp. dried sage

THESE TREATS ARE HIGH-PROTEIN, GRAIN-FREE, AND FILLED WITH OMEGAS.

Preheat oven to 350°. Empty entire cans of salmon (juices included) into a food processor and puree.

Combine all ingredients together (if too dry, add more water, too wet, add a bit more flour). Line a cookie sheet with parchment paper (for easy cleanup), and spoon out mixture with a tablespoon and drop onto sheet (they can be rather close together as they don't grow much while cooking). These cookies will not rise or flatten, so if you want a flatter cookie, press it down before baking.

Bake 22-27 minutes or until golden brown. Transfer and let cool completely on a wire rack. Store the cookies in an airtight container in the refrigerator. For more options, read the "Storage Tips" section on page 18.

SALMON

This delicious, pink-fleshed fish is low in calories and saturated fat, high in protein, and rich in omega-3 fatty acids (the ones that are good for you). Wild-caught cold-water fish, like salmon, are higher in omega-3 fatty acids than warm-water fish. Salmon is also an excellent source of selenium, niacin, and vitamin B12 and a good source of phosphorous, magnesium, and vitamin B6.

BEEF JERKY

{ HOMEMADE BEEF JERKY, SAFE AND TASTY! }

1 lb. boneless top round steak or London broil (trimmed of fat)

THESE TREATS ARE HIGH-PROTEIN
AND GRAIN-FREE.

Place beef in plastic bag or plastic wrap and freeze for 30-60 minutes or until firm but not frozen. This allows for easier slicing on thin strips. Use a sharp knife and slice across the grain into thin strips no more than ¼" thick.

Preheat oven to 250°. Line a cookie sheet with parchment paper (for easy cleanup), and arrange the beef strips in a single layer with a little space between pieces for proper air circulation. Bake for 4 hours, or until dry to the touch. Remove from the oven and let air-dry in a cool place for another 24 hours. Store in an airtight container in the refrigerator.

Yields approximately ¾ lb. jerky.

CHICKEN JERKY

{ HOMEMADE CHICKEN JERKY, SAFE AND TASTY! }

1 lb. boneless skinless chicken breast (trimmed of fat)

THESE TREATS ARE HIGH-PROTEIN
AND GRAIN-FREE.

Place chicken in plastic bag or plastic wrap and freeze for 30 minutes or until firm but not frozen. This allows for easier slicing on thin strips. Use a sharp knife and slice across the grain into thin strips no more than ¼" thick.

Preheat oven to 250°. Line a cookie sheet with parchment paper (for easy cleanup), and arrange the chicken strips in a single layer with a little space between pieces for proper air circulation. Bake for 4 hours, or until dry to the touch. Remove from the oven and let air-dry in a cool place for another 24 hours. Store in an airtight container in the refrigerator.

Yields approximately ¾ lb. jerky.

LIVER ALONE

{ ... BUT NOT IN EXILE }

3 c. amaranth flour (or garbanzo bean flour or tapioca flour)

1 lb. beef livers (or chicken livers)

2 eggs

THESE TREATS ARE HIGH-PROTEIN AND GRAIN-FREE.

Preheat oven to 300°. Puree liver in a food processor. Immediately clean it afterward, as liver makes an awful mess if left in there to dry.

Combine all ingredients together and mix thoroughly. Line a jelly roll pan with parchment paper (it helps make cleanup a breeze). Pour mixture into the pan.

Bake for 30 minutes. Cut into tiny individual-sized portions using a pizza cutter or a knife. Remove from the oven and let cool completely on a wire rack. Store in an airtight container in the refrigerator.

Note: To make crunchier treats, put them back in the oven (after cutting them) for an additional 2 hours at 150°.

GRAIN-FREE FLOURS

Even if your dog isn't gluten intolerant (and be thankful if he isn't), health experts advise going without wheat- and grain-based foods occasionally, and it's helpful to know what to substitute. This recipe is completely grain-free—and your dog won't notice, or care.

JERKY TURKEY

{ ONE TOUGH BIRD, BUT ONE GENTLE-ON-THE-TUMMY TREAT }

....

1 lb. raw ground turkey (or chicken)

1 tbsp. extra-virgin olive oil

>>> • <<<

THESE TREATS ARE HIGH PROTEIN, LOW-FAT, AND GRAIN-FREE.

Preheat oven to 200°. Combine all ingredients together in a food processor and puree the mixture. Line a jelly roll pan with parchment paper (it makes cleanup easier) and pour the mixture into it. Spread evenly.

Bake 2 hours with the oven door slightly ajar to allow the moisture to escape. Remove from oven, and using a pizza cutter or knife, cut into small individual-sized portions. Place pieces back in the oven, flipped over, and bake an additional 1-2 hours or until the treats are dry and leathery. Store in an airtight container in the refrigerator.

GOBBLING UP TURKEY

Turkey is a poultry that is becoming more and more available to consumers because it is naturally low in fat without the skin, containing only 1 gram of fat per ounce of flesh. It is also a good source of B vitamins, potassium, and zinc. Cooked with the skin on, the flavor is sealed in without adding additional fat.

BISON BITES

{ GREAT TO USE AS PURE-MEAT,
HIGH-VALUE TRAINING TREATS }

....

2 lbs. lean ground beef (or buffalo)

---⟩⟩⟩ • ⟨⟨⟨---

THESE TREATS ARE HIGH-PROTEIN, LOW-FAT, AND GRAIN-FREE.

Preheat oven to 200°. Puree the meat in a food processor. Line a jelly roll pan with parchment paper (it makes cleanup easier) and pour the mixture into it. Spread evenly.

Bake 2 hours with the oven door slightly ajar to allow the moisture to escape. Remove from oven and using a pizza cutter or knife cut into small individual sized portions. Place pieces back in the oven, flipped over and bake an additional 1-2 hours or until the treats are dry and leathery. Store in an airtight container in the refrigerator.

HOME ON THE RANGE

Long before settlers moved in and took over, Native Americans were thriving on the multiple blessings of the bison (commonly referred to as the buffalo). One of these was the quality of their meat. In short, bison contains more of what our bodies need—iron, protein, and fatty acids—and less of what we don't (fat, cholesterol, and calories). Because it is nutrient-dense, it can be consumed in smaller quantities than beef and still provide similar (if not increased) health benefits while contributing to a greater feeling of fullness. Nutritionally, you get more protein and nutrients with fewer calories and fat than other protein sources. It is also a less common red meat; if your dog has an allergy to beef, they may quite tolerate to bison.

TUNA SNACKERS

{ A LOW-FAT, ALLERGY FRIENDLY TREAT }

1 ½ c. oat flour

1 ½ c. brown rice flour

6-oz. can albacore tuna (in water)

¼ c. oat bran

1 egg

½ c. water (add slowly)

THESE TREATS ARE HIGH-PROTEIN, LOW-FAT, ALLERGY-FRIENDLY, AND FILLED WITH BENEFICIAL OMEGAS.

Preheat oven to 350°. Empty all contents (including juices) from can of tuna into a food processor and puree.

Combine all ingredients (except the water) together. Add water slowly and mix until a dough forms (if too dry, add more water, too wet, add a bit more flour). You may not need all the water if you reach a good consistency first. Roll out on a lightly floured surface to

¼" thickness. Use a cookie cutter (or a knife) to cut into shapes. Line a cookie sheet with parchment paper (for easy cleanup), and place the cookies on the sheet (they can be rather close together as they don't grow much while cooking).

Bake 22-27 minutes or until golden brown. Transfer and let cool completely on a wire rack. Store the cookies in an airtight container in the refrigerator. For more options, read the "Storage Tips" section on page 18.

LAMB LOVIES

{ GRAIN-FREE LAMB TREAT PERFECT FOR DOGS THAT SUFFER WITH A LOT OF ALLERGIES }

2 c. pumpkin or sweet potato (canned or fresh)

3 c. garbanzo bean flour (or tapioca flour, or amaranth flour)

1 c. ground lamb (cooked and drained)

1 tsp. rosemary

1 tsp. sage

½ c. water (add slowly)

THESE TREATS ARE HIGH-PROTEIN, GRAIN-FREE, AND ALLERGY FRIENDLY.

Preheat oven to 350°. If using fresh pumpkin or sweet potato, cook, mash, and puree.

Combine all ingredients together (if too dry, add more water, too wet, add a bit more flour). Line a cookie sheet with parchment paper (for easy cleanup), and spoon out mixture with a tablespoon and drop onto sheet (they can be rather close together as they don't grow much while cooking). These cookies will not rise or flatten, so if you want a flatter cookie, press it down before baking.

Bake 22-27 minutes or until golden brown. Transfer and let cool completely on a wire rack. Store the cookies in an airtight container in the refrigerator. For more options, read the "Storage Tips" section on page 18.

HERBS FOR LIFE

Whole books have been written on herbs and their health benefits. Sidebars in other chapters of this book have detailed the benefits of some of those most commonly used in dog food (and specifically the treats in this book!). Two particularly interesting websites to visit to learn more include www.crystalgardenherbs.com and www.botanicalmedicine.org.

MINTY FRESH

{ HELPS TO FRESHEN UP BAD BREATH! }

1 ½ c. oat flour

1 ½ c. brown rice flour

¼ c. applesauce (unsweetened)

½ c. dried mint

½ c. dried parsley

¼ tsp. peppermint oil

1 egg

½ c. water (add slowly)

Preheat oven to 350°. Combine all ingredients together (if too dry, add more water, too wet, add a bit more flour). Line a cookie sheet with parchment paper (for easy cleanup), and spoon out mixture with a tablespoon and drop onto sheet (they can be rather close together as they don't grow much while cooking). These cookies will not rise or flatten, so if you want a flatter cookie, press it down before baking. Bake 22-27 minutes or until golden brown. Transfer and let cool completely on a wire rack. Store the cookies in an airtight container in the refrigerator. For more options, read the "Storage Tips" section on page 18.

TURKEY BREAST JERKY

{ HIGH-PROTEIN, LOW-FAT, GRAIN-FREE }

....

2 lbs. turkey breast (boneless, skinless)

—————»» • ««—————

Put turkey in the freezer for 30 minutes to allow it to become more firm.

Slice the breast thinly, about ⅛" slices, cutting against the grain (that will make the jerky a little harder to chew and give your dog more time eating it). Try to keep the slices as uniform as possible, so the cook time stays consistent.

Preheat oven to 175°. Put a wire drying rack on top of a pan, then place the turkey slices on top of the wire rack. Do not overlap the pieces. Bake for 2 hours, then flip the strips, and bake another 2 hours. If you want to make the jerky even chewier, cook additional time, until the desired consistency is reached. Store in an airtight container in the refrigerator.

LIVER JERKY

{ HIGH-VALUE TREAT, GREAT FOR TRAINING }

2 lbs. chicken livers

Put chicken livers in the freezer for 20 minutes to allow it them to become firmer. Slice the livers thinly, about $1/8"$ slices. Try to keep the slices as uniform as possible, so the cook time stays consistent.

Preheat oven to 175°. Put a wire drying rack on top of a pan, then place the turkey slices on top of the wire rack. Do not overlap the pieces. Bake for 2 hours, then flip the strips, and bake another 1-2 hours. These are smaller bite sized pieces, so they are great for training. If you wanted to make larger liver jerky, you can use beef liver, since they are much bigger in size. Store in an airtight container in the refrigerator.

SALMON JERKY

{ FULL OF OMEGAS, HEART, SKIN & COAT HEALTHY }

2 lbs. salmon fillets (skin-on preferred)

Put salmon in the freezer for 30 minutes to allow it them to become firmer. Slice the fillets thinly, about ⅛" slices, keeping the skin on. Cut against the grain, to make the jerky chewier for your dog. Try to keep the slices as uniform as possible, so the cook time stays consistent.

Preheat oven to 175°. Put a wire drying rack on top of a pan, then place the salmon slices on top of the wire rack. Do not overlap the pieces. Bake for 2 hours, then flip the strips, and bake another 2 hours. These are smaller bite sized pieces, so they are great for training. If you wanted to make larger liver jerky, you can use beef liver, since they are much bigger in size. Store in an airtight container in the refrigerator.

SWEET POTATO CHEWS
{ LOW-PROTEIN, HIGH-FIBER, GREAT FOR SENSITIVE BELLIES }

2 sweet potatoes

For smaller dogs, slice the sweet potato in rounds, about $^1/_4$" thick, keeping the skin on. For larger dogs, slice them into $^1/_4$" strips, lengthwise. Try to keep the slices as uniform as possible, so the cook time stays consistent.

Preheat oven to 250°. Place slices on a baking sheet lined with parchment. Do not overlap the pieces. Bake for 1.5 hours, then flip the pieces, and bake another 1-1.5 hours. The longer they stay in the oven, the crispier they'll get, the shorter they stay in, the chewier they'll be. Store in an airtight container in the refrigerator.

PIG SKIN JERKY

{ YOUR DOG WILL GO CRAZY FOR THESE! }

2 lbs. pig skin

→→⟩⟩⟩ • ⟨⟨⟨←←

You can buy sliced pig skin in most supermarkets' meat section, and it makes a great treat for your dogs, one that is sure to become a favorite. Slice the skin into evenly sized strips, keeping in mind the size of your dog (we recommend 2" x 6" for medium to larger sized dogs, and smaller for smaller dogs). Try to keep the slices as uniform as possible, so the cook time stays consistent.

Preheat oven to 175°. Put a wire drying rack on top of a pan, then place the strips on top of the wire rack. Do not overlap the pieces. Bake for 5 hours, then flip the strips, and bake another 5 hours. The time will vary depending upon how thick the skins were cut, how much fat was on them and how crunchy you want them to be. We recommend staying pretty crunchy, but still a bit chewy for a longer lasting treat. Store in an airtight container in the refrigerator.

DRIED APPLE CHEWS

{ LOW-FAT, LOW-PROTEIN, HIGH-FIBER SNACKS }

3 apples (Gala, Fuji, Honeycrisp, or Granny Smith)

Remove the core and seeds (apple seeds can be toxic to dogs), then slice the apples into $1/4$" rounds. Try to keep the slices as uniform as possible, so the cook time stays consistent.

Preheat oven to 200°. Place slices on a baking sheet lined with parchment. Do not overlap the pieces. Bake for 1.5 hours, then flip the pieces, and bake another 1 hour. The longer they stay in the oven, the crispier they'll get, the shorter they stay in, the chewier they'll be. Store in an airtight container in the refrigerator.

LAMB JERKY

{ HIGH-PROTEIN, LOW-FAT, GRAIN-FREE, ALTERNATIVE PROTEIN SOURCE }

2 lbs. lamb loin or fillet

Put lamb in the freezer for 30 minutes to allow it to become firmer. Slice the loin thinly, about $1/8$" slices, cutting against the grain. Try to keep the slices as uniform as possible, so the cook time stays consistent.

Preheat oven to 175°. Put a wire drying rack on top of a pan, then place the lamb slices on top of the wire rack. Do not overlap the pieces. Bake for 2 hours, then flip the strips, and bake another 2 hours. If you want to make the jerky even chewier, cook additional time, until the desired consistency is reached. Store in an airtight container in the refrigerator.

KALE CHIPS

{ LOW-FAT, HIGH-FIBER SNACKS,
DOGS LIKE KALE TOO! }

1 bag or bunch of fresh kale

2 tbsp. coconut oil

Wash kale, then tear the leaves into bite-sized pieces and place in a large mixing bowl. Toss with the coconut oil to evenly coat.

Preheat oven to 350°. Place leaves on a baking sheet lined with parchment. Do not overlap the pieces. Bake for 12-16 minutes. The leaves should still be dark green and not burnt or brown looking. Let cool completely. Store in an airtight container in the refrigerator.

STRAWBERRY-APPLE FRUIT LEATHER

{ HIGH-FIBER, LOW-FAT, GREAT FOR SENSITIVE TUMMIES }

1 c. applesauce (unsweetened)

2 c. strawberries (fresh or frozen)

⟶⟫⟶ • ⟵⟪⟵

Place all ingredients in a blender or food processor and puree.

Preheat oven to 175°. Line a baking sheet with parchment paper and then spread the mixture out evenly in the pan using a spatula. Bake for 6 hours, then remove from the oven, leave the pan on the counter to cool an additional 4 hours (or overnight). Use kitchen scissors to cut the fruit leather into strips (you can leave the parchment paper on at this time and remove it later when you go to feed it to your dog). Store in an airtight container in the refrigerator.

CHAPTER 7

VEGETARIAN & VEGAN

High-fiber & low-protein treats

Now, we know dogs love meat, but they also love fruits and veggies. There are a lot of reasons why, as an owner, you would chose to feed your dog a vegetarian or vegan treat. Maybe they are overweight, and the doctor prescribed more veggies in their diet, or they need more fiber in their diet to regulate their stool. Maybe you chose to feed more vegetarian or vegan treats as it aligns with your own lifestyle choices, or maybe the dog has liver or kidney ailments and the doctor has recommended a low-protein diet.

SWEET POTATO / FLAX SEED

{ HIGH-FIBER, LOW-PROTEIN, GREAT FOR SENSITIVE TUMMIES & DIGESTIVE HEALTH }

1 ½ c. oat flour

1 ½ c. brown rice flour

½ c. pureed sweet potato (canned or fresh)

1 large, ripe banana (mashed)

½ tsp. ground cinnamon

⅓ c. water (add slowly)

Preheat the oven to 350°. Combine all ingredients (except the water) together. Add water slowly and mix until a dough forms (if too dry, add more water, too wet, add a bit more flour). You may not need all the water to reach the desired consistency. Use a cookie cutter (or a knife) to cut into shapes. Roll out on a lightly floured surface to ¼" thickness. Line a cookie sheet with parchment paper (for easy cleanup) and place the cookies on the sheet (they can be rather close together as they don't expand much while cooking).

Bake 18-25 minutes or until golden brown. Transfer and let cool completely on a wire rack. Store the cookies in an airtight container in the refrigerator. For more options, read the "Storage Tips" section on page 18.

RASPBERRY / APPLE / ALMOND

{ ANTIOXIDANT-RICH & HIGH IN FIBER }

....

1 1/2 c. oat flour

1 1/2 c. brown rice flour

1/2 c. almond butter (unsalted, natural is best)

1/2 c. pureed raspberries (frozen or fresh)

1/2 c. applesauce (unsweetened)

1/3 c. water (add slowly)

⟶⟶⟶ • ⟵⟵⟵

Preheat oven to 375°. Combine all ingredients (except the water) together. Add water slowly and mix until a dough forms (if too dry, add more water, too wet, add a bit more flour). You may not need all the water to reach the desired consistency. Use a cookie cutter (or a knife) to cut into shapes. Roll out on a lightly floured surface to 1/4" thickness. Line a cookie sheet with parchment paper (for easy cleanup) and place the cookies on the sheet (they can be rather close together as they don't expand much while cooking).

Bake 18-25 minutes or until golden brown. Transfer and let cool completely on a wire rack. Store the cookies in an airtight container in the refrigerator. For more options, read the "Storage Tips" section on page 18.

STRAWBERRY / BANANA

{ HIGH-FIBER & LOW-PROTEIN
AND FULL OF NUTRIENTS }

1 ½ c. oat flour

1 ½ c. brown rice flour

½ c. pureed strawberries (fresh or frozen)

1 large, ripe banana (mashed)

1 tbsp. honey

⅓ c. water (add slowly)

Preheat the oven to 350°. Combine all ingredients (except the water) together. Add water slowly and mix until a dough forms (if too dry, add more water, too wet, add a bit more flour). You may not need all the water to reach the desired consistency. Use a cookie cutter (or a knife) to cut into shapes. Roll out on a lightly floured surface to ¼" thickness. Line a cookie sheet with parchment paper (for easy cleanup) and place the cookies on the sheet (they can be rather close together as they don't expand much while cooking).

Bake 18-25 minutes or until golden brown. Transfer and let cool completely on a wire rack. Store the cookies in an airtight container in the refrigerator. For more options, read the "Storage Tips" section on page 18.

PUMPKIN /
PEANUT BUTTER

{ HIGH-FIBER & GREAT FOR DIGESTIVE HEALTH }

1 ½ c. oat flour

1 ½ c. brown rice flour

½ c. peanut butter (unsalted, natural is best)

½ c. pureed pumpkin (canned or fresh)

½ c. water (add slowly)

Preheat oven to 375°. Combine all ingredients (except the water) together. Add water slowly and mix until a dough forms (if too dry, add more water, too wet, add a bit more flour). You may not need all the water to reach the desired consistency. Use a cookie cutter (or a knife) to cut into shapes. Roll out on a lightly floured surface to ¼" thickness. Line a cookie sheet with parchment paper (for easy cleanup) and place the cookies on the sheet (they can be rather close together as they don't expand much while cooking).

Bake 18-25 minutes or until golden brown. Transfer and let cool completely on a wire rack. Store the cookies in an airtight container in the refrigerator. For more options, read the "Storage Tips" section on page 18.

BLUEBERRY / OATS

{ HIGH-FIBER, LOW-PROTEIN & ANTIOXIDANT-RICH }

....

1 1/2 c. oat flour

1 1/2 c. brown rice flour

1/2 c. pureed blueberries (fresh or frozen)

1 large, ripe banana (mashed)

1/2 c. old-fashioned oats

2 tbsp. flax seeds

2 tbsp. coconut oil

1/2 c. water (add slowly)

Preheat the oven to 350°. Combine all ingredients (except the water) together. Add water slowly and mix until a dough forms (if too dry, add more water, too wet, add a bit more flour). You may not need all the water to reach the desired consistency. Use a cookie cutter (or a knife) to cut into shapes. Roll out on a lightly floured surface to 1/4" thickness. Line a cookie sheet with parchment paper (for easy cleanup) and place the cookies on the sheet (they can be rather close together as they don't expand much while cooking).

Bake 18-25 minutes or until golden brown. Transfer and let cool completely on a wire rack. Store the cookies in an airtight container in the refrigerator. For more options, read the "Storage Tips" section on page 18.

KALE / COCONUT / TURMERIC

{ HIGH-FIBER, LOW-PROTEIN, GREAT FOR SKIN, COAT & INFLAMMATION ISSUES }

1 ½ c. oat flour

1 ½ c. brown rice flour

1 c. tightly packed kale leaves (pureed)

½ tsp. ground turmeric

¼ c. coconut oil

¼ c. water (add slowly)

Preheat the oven to 350°. Combine all ingredients (except the water) together. Add water slowly and mix until a dough forms (if too dry, add more water, too wet, add a bit more flour). You may not need all the water to reach the desired consistency. Use a cookie cutter (or a knife) to cut into shapes. Roll out on a lightly floured surface to ¼" thickness. Line a cookie sheet with parchment paper (for easy cleanup) and place the cookies on the sheet (they can be rather close together as they don't expand much while cooking).

Bake 18-25 minutes or until golden brown. Transfer and let cool completely on a wire rack. Store the cookies in an airtight container in the refrigerator. For more options, read the "Storage Tips" section on page 18.

PUMPKIN / CARROT / APPLE

{ HIGH-FIBER, LOW-PROTEIN & FULL OF VITAMINS }

1 ½ c. oat flour

1 ½ c. brown rice flour

½ c. pureed pumpkin (canned or fresh)

½ c. pureed carrots

½ c. applesauce (unsweetened)

Preheat the oven to 350°. Combine all ingredients together. If too dry, add 1 tablespoon of water at a time to reach desired consistency. If it gets too wet, add more flour. Use a cookie cutter (or a knife) to cut into shapes. Roll out on a lightly floured surface to ¼" thickness. Line a cookie sheet with parchment paper (for easy cleanup) and place the cookies on the sheet (they can be rather close together as they don't expand much while cooking).

Bake 18-25 minutes or until golden brown. Transfer and let cool completely on a wire rack. Store the cookies in an airtight container in the refrigerator. For more options, read the "Storage Tips" section on page 18.

CRANBERRY / COCONUT

{ ANTIOXIDANT-RICH, LOW-PROTEIN, GREAT FOR SKIN, COAT & KIDNEY HEALTH }

1 ½ c. oat flour

1 ½ c. brown rice flour

½ c. dried cranberries

½ c. shredded coconut (unsweetened)

1 large, ripe banana (mashed)

2 tbsp. coconut oil

½ c. coconut water (add slowly)

Preheat the oven to 350°. Combine all ingredients (except the coconut water) together. Add water slowly and mix until a dough forms (if too dry, add more coconut water, too wet, add a bit more flour). You may not need all the coconut water to reach the desired consistency. Use a cookie cutter (or a knife) to cut into shapes. Roll out on a lightly floured surface to ¼" thickness. Line a cookie sheet with parchment paper (for easy cleanup) and place the cookies on the sheet (they can be rather close together as they don't expand much while cooking).

Bake 18-25 minutes or until golden brown. Transfer and let cool completely on a wire rack. Store the cookies in an airtight container in the refrigerator. For more options, read the "Storage Tips" section on page 18.

KALE / SWEET POTATO

{ HIGH-FIBER, LOW-PROTEIN, GREAT FOR SKIN, COAT & SENSITIVE BELLIES }

1 $\frac{1}{2}$ c. oat flour

1 $\frac{1}{2}$ c. brown rice flour

1 c. tightly packed kale leaves (pureed)

1 c. pureed sweet potato (fresh or canned)

2 tbsp. flax seeds

$\frac{1}{4}$ c. coconut oil

$\frac{1}{4}$ c. water (add slowly)

Preheat the oven to 350°. Combine all ingredients (except the water) together. Add water slowly and mix until a dough forms (if too dry, add more water, too wet, add a bit more flour). You may not need all the water to reach the desired consistency. Use a cookie cutter (or a knife) to cut into shapes. Roll out on a lightly floured surface to $\frac{1}{4}$" thickness. Line a cookie sheet with parchment paper (for easy cleanup) and place the cookies on the sheet (they can be rather close together as they don't expand much while cooking).

Bake 18-25 minutes or until golden brown. Transfer and let cool completely on a wire rack. Store the cookies in an airtight container in the refrigerator. For more options, read the "Storage Tips" section on page 18.

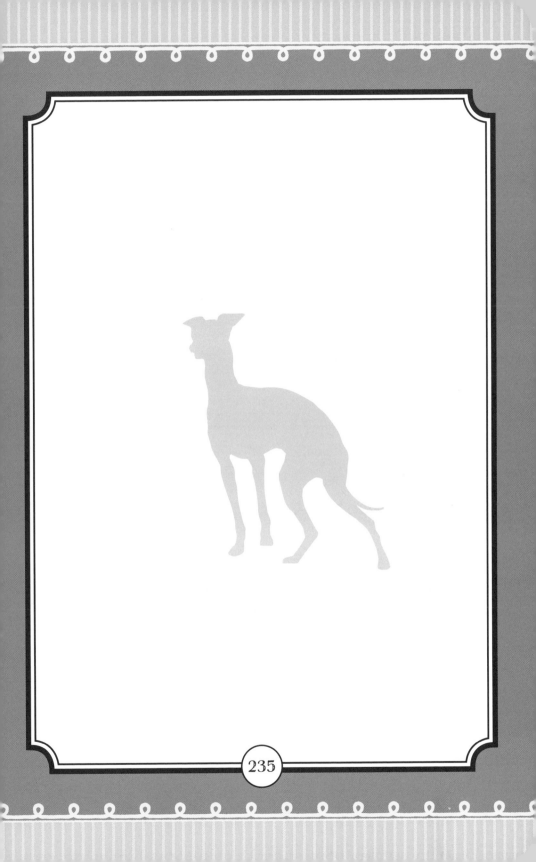

PEANUT BUTTER / BANANA / BERRY

{ ANTIOXIDANT-RICH, FULL OF VITAMINS,
AND A TASTE DOGS LOVE }

1 $\frac{1}{2}$ c. oat flour

1 $\frac{1}{2}$ c. brown rice flour

$\frac{1}{2}$ c. pureed blueberries (fresh or frozen)

$\frac{1}{2}$ c. peanut butter (unsalted)

1 large, ripe banana (mashed)

1 tbsp. honey

$\frac{1}{2}$ tsp. ground cinnamon

$\frac{1}{3}$ c. water (add slowly)

Preheat the oven to 350°. Combine all ingredients (except the water) together. Add water slowly and mix until a dough forms (if too dry, add more water, too wet, add a bit more flour). You may not need all the water to reach the desired consistency. Use a cookie cutter (or a knife) to cut into shapes. Roll out on a lightly floured surface to $\frac{1}{4}$" thickness. Line a cookie sheet with parchment paper (for easy cleanup) and place the cookies on the sheet (they can be rather close together as they don't expand much while cooking).

Bake 18-25 minutes or until golden brown. Transfer and let cool completely on a wire rack. Store the cookies in an airtight container in the refrigerator. For more options, read the "Storage Tips" section on page 18.

CHAPTER 8

QUICK & EASY

5 ingredients or less

We know you're busy, who isn't?! But we also know you want to feel good knowing you're making a healthy, homemade treat for your dog. That's why we created this chapter, filled with 20 recipes, all containing 5 ingredients or less* (many of which you likely already have in your kitchen), all quick and easy, and also made with nutrient-rich, healthy, and beneficial ingredients. Oh, and your dog's going to be drooling at the smell of them.

Note: As water is needed in varying amounts, and is so readily available, it is not counted among the ingredients.

238

BONE BROTH / TURMERIC

{ NUTRIENT-DENSE, EASY & HEALTHY }

1 ½ c. oat flour

1 ½ c. brown rice flour

1 tsp. ground turmeric

1 egg

½ c. bone broth (add slowly)

Preheat the oven to 350°. Combine all ingredients (except the broth) together. Add broth slowly and mix until a dough forms (if too dry, add more broth, too wet, add a bit more oat flour). You may not need all of the broth to reach the desired consistency. Use a cookie cutter (or a knife) to cut into shapes. Roll out on a lightly floured surface to ¼" thickness. Line a cookie sheet with parchment paper (for easy cleanup) and place the cookies on the sheet (they can be rather close together, as they don't expand much while cooking).

Bake 22-27 minutes or until golden brown. Transfer and let cool completely on a wire rack. Store the cookies in an airtight container in the refrigerator. For more options, read the "Storage Tips" section on page 18.

Note: We recommend using beef bone broth (you can make it yourself with your leftover bones or ones you buy from the butcher, or you can purchase premade bone broth). You can also use poultry, pork, bison, or lamb broth for these tasty biscuits.

PEANUT BUTTER / BANANA

{ SO TASTY, YOU'RE GONNA WANT SOME, TOO }

1 ½ c. oat flour

1 ½ c. brown rice flour

½ c. peanut butter

1 large banana (extra ripe, mashed)

½ c. water (add slowly)

Preheat oven to 375°. Combine all ingredients (except the water) together. Add water slowly and mix until a dough forms (if too dry, add more water, too wet, add a bit more flour). You may not need all the water to reach the desired consistency. Use a cookie cutter (or a knife) to cut the dough into the desired shapes. Roll out on a lightly floured surface to ¼" thickness. Line a cookie sheet with parchment paper (for easy cleanup) and place the cookies on the sheet (they can be rather close together as they don't expand much while cooking).

Bake 18-25 minutes or until golden brown. Transfer and let cool completely on a wire rack. Store the cookies in an airtight container in the refrigerator. For more options, read the "Storage Tips" section on page 18.

CHICKEN / BASIL

{ PROTEIN-RICH & ANTIVIRAL, OH, AND GREAT SMELLING }

1 ½ c. oat flour

1 ½ c. brown rice flour

½ c. ground chicken (cooked)

1 tbsp. ground basil

1 egg

½ c. water (add slowly)

Preheat the oven to 350°. Combine all ingredients (except the water) together. Add water slowly and mix until a dough forms (if too dry, add more water, too wet, add a bit more flour). You may not need all the water to reach the desired consistency. Use a cookie cutter (or a knife) to cut the dough into the desired shapes. Roll out on a lightly floured surface to ¼" thickness. Line a cookie sheet with parchment paper (for easy cleanup) and place the cookies on the sheet (they can be rather close together as they don't expand much while cooking).

Bake 22-27 minutes or until golden brown. Transfer and let cool completely on a wire rack. Store the cookies in an airtight container in the refrigerator. For more options, read the "Storage Tips" section on page 18.

BLUEBERRY / ALMOND

{ ANTIOXIDANT-RICH, TASTY & VEGETARIAN }

....

1 1/2 c. oat flour

1 1/2 c. brown rice flour

1/2 c. almond butter (unsalted, natural is best)

1/2 c. pureed blueberries (frozen or fresh)

1/2 c. water (add slowly)

Preheat oven to 375°. Combine all ingredients (except the water) together. Add water slowly and mix until a dough forms (if too dry, add more water, too wet, add a bit more flour). You may not need all the water to reach the desired consistency. Use a cookie cutter (or a knife) to cut the dough into the desired shapes. Roll out on a lightly floured surface to 1/4" thickness. Line a cookie sheet with parchment paper (for easy cleanup) and place the cookies on the sheet (they can be rather close together as they don't expand much while cooking).

Bake 18-25 minutes or until golden brown. Transfer and let cool completely on a wire rack. Store the cookies in an airtight container in the refrigerator. For more options, read the "Storage Tips" section on page 18.

TURKEY / CARROT

{ LOW-FAT, HIGH-FIBER, AND SUPER TASTY }

....

1 ½ c. oat flour

1 ½ c. brown rice flour

½ c. ground turkey (cooked)

½ c. pureed carrots

1 egg

½ c. water (add slowly)

Preheat the oven to 350°. Combine all ingredients (except the water) together. Add water slowly and mix until a dough forms (if too dry, add more water, too wet, add a bit more flour). You may not need all the water to reach the desired consistency. Use a cookie cutter (or a knife) to cut the dough into the desired shapes. Roll out on a lightly floured surface to ¼" thickness. Line a cookie sheet with parchment paper (for easy cleanup) and place the cookies on the sheet (they can be rather close together as they don't expand much while cooking).

Bake 22-27 minutes or until golden brown. Transfer and let cool completely on a wire rack. Store the cookies in an airtight container in the refrigerator. For more options, read the "Storage Tips" section on page 18.

PUMPKIN / HONEY

{ HIGH IN FIBER AND GREAT FOR SENSITIVE TUMMIES }

1 ½ c. oat flour

1 ½ c. brown rice flour

½ c. pureed pumpkin (canned or fresh)

1 tbsp. honey

½ c. water (add slowly)

$$\longrightarrow\!\!\!\!\gg\!\!\cdot\!\!\ll\!\!\!\!\longleftarrow$$

Preheat oven to 375°. Combine all ingredients (except the water) together. Add water slowly and mix until a dough forms (if too dry, add more water, too wet, add a bit more flour). You may not need all the water to reach the desired consistency. Use a cookie cutter (or a knife) to cut the dough into the desired shapes. Roll out on a lightly floured surface to ¼" thickness. Line a cookie sheet with parchment paper (for easy cleanup), and place the cookies on the sheet (they can be rather close together as they don't expand much while cooking).

Bake 18-25 minutes or until golden brown. Transfer and let cool completely on a wire rack. Store the cookies in an airtight container in the refrigerator. For more options, read the "Storage Tips" section on page 18.

BEEF / PARSLEY

{ RICH IN PROTEIN & BREATH-FRESHENING }

1 ½ c. oat flour

1 ½ c. brown rice flour

½ c. ground beef (cooked)

2 tbsp. ground parsley

1 egg

½ c. water (add slowly)

Preheat the oven to 350°. Combine all ingredients (except the water) together. Add water slowly and mix until a dough forms (if too dry, add more water, too wet, add a bit more flour). You may not need all the water to reach the desired consistency. Use a cookie cutter (or a knife) to cut the dough into the desired shapes. Roll out on a lightly floured surface to ¼" thickness. Line a cookie sheet with parchment paper (for easy cleanup), and place the cookies on the sheet (they can be rather close together as they don't expand much while cooking).

Bake 22-27 minutes or until golden brown. Transfer and let cool completely on a wire rack. Store the cookies in an airtight container in the refrigerator. For more options, read the "Storage Tips" section on page 18.

APPLE / CINNAMON

{ FULL OF VITAMINS & LOW-PROTEIN, GREAT FOR KIDNEY OR LIVER AILMENTS }

1 ½ c. oat flour

1 ½ c. brown rice flour

½ c. applesauce (unsweetened)

1 tsp. ground cinnamon

½ c. water (add slowly)

Preheat oven to 375°. Combine all ingredients (except the water) together. Add water slowly and mix until a dough forms (if too dry, add more water, too wet, add a bit more flour). You may not need all the water to reach the desired consistency. Use a cookie cutter (or a knife) to cut the dough into the desired shapes. Roll out on a lightly floured surface to ¼" thickness. Line a cookie sheet with parchment paper (for easy cleanup) and place the cookies on the sheet (they can be rather close together as they don't expand much while cooking).

Bake 18-25 minutes or until golden brown. Transfer and let cool completely on a wire rack. Store the cookies in an airtight container in the refrigerator. For more options, read the "Storage Tips" section on page 18.

SALMON /
SWEET POTATO

{ OMEGA-RICH & GREAT FOR SKIN, COAT & HEART HEALTH }

1 ½ c. oat flour

1 ½ c. brown rice flour

6-oz. can wild-caught salmon

½ c. pureed sweet potato (canned or fresh)

1 egg

½ c. water (add slowly)

Preheat the oven to 350°. Combine all ingredients (except the water) together, and use all the liquid from the can of salmon, dogs love that! Add water slowly and mix until a dough forms (if too dry, add more water, too wet, add a bit more flour). You may not need all the water to reach the desired consistency. Use a cookie cutter (or a knife) to cut the dough into the desired shapes. Roll out on a lightly floured surface to ¼" thickness. Line a cookie sheet with parchment paper (for easy cleanup), and place the cookies on the sheet (they can be rather close together as they don't expand much while cooking).

Bake 22-27 minutes or until golden brown. Transfer and let cool completely on a wire rack. Store the cookies in an airtight container in the refrigerator. For more options, read the "Storage Tips" section on page 18.

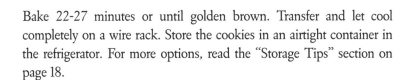

PEANUT BUTTER / BACON

{ THESE MIGHT BE DOGS FAVORITE TWO INGREDIENTS, THIS WILL BE A GO-TO RECIPE }

1 ½ c. oat flour

1 ½ c. brown rice flour

½ c. peanut butter (unsalted, natural)

6 slices of cooked bacon (ground)

½ c. water (add slowly)

Preheat oven to 375˚. Combine all ingredients (except the water) together. Add water slowly and mix until a dough forms (if too dry, add more water, too wet, add a bit more flour). You may not need all the water to reach the desired consistency. Use a cookie cutter (or a knife) to cut the dough into the desired shapes. Roll out on a lightly floured surface to ¼" thickness. Line a cookie sheet with parchment paper (for easy cleanup) and place the cookies on the sheet (they can be rather close together as they don't expand much while cooking).

Bake 18-25 minutes or until golden brown. Transfer and let cool completely on a wire rack. Store the cookies in an airtight container in the refrigerator. For more options, read the "Storage Tips" section on page 18.

MOZZARELLA / OREGANO

{ COME ON, WHOSE DOG DOESN'T LOVE PIZZA CRUSTS?! }

1 ½ c. oat flour

1 ½ c. brown rice flour

½ c. mozzarella cheese (shredded)

1 tbsp. ground oregano

1 egg

½ c. water (add slowly)

Preheat the oven to 350°. Combine all ingredients (except the water) together. Add water slowly and mix until a dough forms (if too dry, add more water, too wet, add a bit more flour). You may not need all the water to reach the desired consistency. Use a cookie cutter (or a knife) to cut the dough into the desired shapes. Roll out on a lightly floured surface to ¼" thickness. Line a cookie sheet with parchment paper (for easy cleanup) and place the cookies on the sheet (they can be rather close together as they don't expand much while cooking).

Bake 22-27 minutes or until golden brown. Transfer and let cool completely on a wire rack. Store the cookies in an airtight container in the refrigerator. For more options, read the "Storage Tips" section on page 18.

CRANBERRY / PUMPKIN

{ HIGH IN FIBER, ANTIOXIDANT-RICH & GREAT FOR KIDNEY HEALTH }

1 ½ c. oat flour

1 ½ c. brown rice flour

½ c. pureed pumpkin (canned or fresh)

½ c. dried cranberries (pureed)

½ c. water (add slowly)

⟫⟫⟩ • ⟨⟨⟨

Preheat oven to 375°. Combine all ingredients (except the water) together. Add water slowly and mix until a dough forms (if too dry, add more water, too wet, add a bit more flour). You may not need all the water to reach the desired consistency. Use a cookie cutter (or a knife) to cut the dough into the desired shapes. Roll out on a lightly floured surface to ¼" thickness. Line a cookie sheet with parchment paper (for easy cleanup) and place the cookies on the sheet (they can be rather close together as they don't expand much while cooking).

Bake 18-25 minutes or until golden brown. Transfer and let cool completely on a wire rack. Store the cookies in an airtight container in the refrigerator. For more options, read the "Storage Tips" section on page 18.

LIVER / FLAX SEEDS

{ HIGH IN PROTEIN, VITAMINS, MINERALS & OMEGAS }

1 ½ c. oat flour

1 ½ c. brown rice flour

½ c. raw beef or chicken liver (pureed)

2 tbsp. flax seeds

1 egg

½ c. water (add slowly)

Preheat the oven to 350°. Combine all ingredients (except the water) together. Add water slowly and mix until a dough forms (if too dry, add more water, too wet, add a bit more flour). You may not need all the water to reach the desired consistency. Use a cookie cutter (or a knife) to cut the dough into the desired shapes. Roll out on a lightly floured surface to ¼" thickness. Line a cookie sheet with parchment paper (for easy cleanup) and place the cookies on the sheet (they can be rather close together as they don't expand much while cooking).

Bake 22-27 minutes or until golden brown. Transfer and let cool completely on a wire rack. Store the cookies in an airtight container in the refrigerator. For more options, read the "Storage Tips" section on page 18.

Note: Liver is not the best-smelling meat, so we highly recommend you wash your food processor right after pureeing the liver.

COCONUT /
PEANUT BUTTER

{ GREAT FOR SKIN, COAT & DIGESTIVE HEALTH, AND OH, SO TASTY }

1 $\frac{1}{2}$ c. oat flour

1 $\frac{1}{2}$ c. brown rice flour

$\frac{1}{2}$ c. peanut butter (unsalted, natural)

$\frac{1}{4}$ c. coconut oil

$\frac{1}{4}$ c. water (add slowly)

Preheat oven to 375°. Combine all ingredients (except the water) together. Add water slowly and mix until a dough forms (if too dry, add more water, too wet, add a bit more flour). You may not need all the water to reach the desired consistency. Use a cookie cutter (or a knife) to cut the dough into the desired shapes. Roll out on a lightly floured surface to $\frac{1}{4}$" thickness. Line a cookie sheet with parchment paper (for easy cleanup) and place the cookies on the sheet (they can be rather close together as they don't expand much while cooking).

Bake 18-25 minutes or until golden brown. Transfer and let cool completely on a wire rack. Store the cookies in an airtight container in the refrigerator. For more options, read the "Storage Tips" section on page 18.

BACON / CHEDDAR

{ THIS IS AN ALL-TIME DOG FAVORITE, YOU CAN'T GO WRONG HERE }

1 ½ c. oat flour

1 ½ c. brown rice flour

6 slices of cooked bacon (ground)

½ c. cheddar cheese (shredded)

1 egg

½ c. water (add slowly)

Preheat the oven to 350°. Combine all ingredients (except the water) together. Add water slowly and mix until a dough forms (if too dry, add more water, too wet, add a bit more flour). You may not need all the water to reach the desired consistency. Use a cookie cutter (or a knife) to cut the dough into the desired shapes. Roll out on a lightly floured surface to ¼" thickness. Line a cookie sheet with parchment paper (for easy cleanup) and place the cookies on the sheet (they can be rather close together as they don't expand much while cooking).

Bake 22-27 minutes or until golden brown. Transfer and let cool completely on a wire rack. Store the cookies in an airtight container in the refrigerator. For more options, read the "Storage Tips" section on page 18.

SWEET POTATO / APPLE

{ HIGH IN FIBER, POTASSIUM & ANTIOXIDANTS, LOW IN PROTEIN }

1 1/2 c. oat flour

1 1/2 c. brown rice flour

1/2 c. pureed sweet potato (canned or fresh)

1/2 c. applesauce (unsweetened)

1 egg

Preheat the oven to 375°. Combine all ingredients together. Mix until a dough forms (if too dry, add 1 tablespoon water of water at a time, too wet, add a bit more flour). Use a cookie cutter (or a knife) to cut the dough into the desired shapes. Roll out on a lightly floured surface to 1/4" thickness. Line a cookie sheet with parchment paper (for easy cleanup) and place the cookies on the sheet (they can be rather close together as they don't expand much while cooking).

Bake 18-25 minutes or until golden brown. Transfer and let cool completely on a wire rack. Store the cookies in an airtight container in the refrigerator. For more options, read the "Storage Tips" section on page 18.

LAMB / MINT

{ A GREAT ALTERNATIVE PROTEIN SOURCE & BREATH-FRESHENING }

1 ½ c. oat flour

1 ½ c. brown rice flour

½ c. ground lamb (cooked)

¼ c. fresh mint leaves (finely chopped)

1 egg

½ c. water (add slowly)

Preheat the oven to 350°. Combine all ingredients (except the water) together. Add water slowly and mix until a dough forms (if too dry, add more water, too wet, add a bit more flour). You may not need all the water to reach the desired consistency. Use a cookie cutter (or a knife) to cut the dough into the desired shapes. Roll out on a lightly floured surface to ¼" thickness. Line a cookie sheet with parchment paper (for easy cleanup) and place the cookies on the sheet (they can be rather close together as they don't expand much while cooking).

Bake 22-27 minutes or until golden brown. Transfer and let cool completely on a wire rack. Store the cookies in an airtight container in the refrigerator. For more options, read the "Storage Tips" section on page 18.

KALE / PUMPKIN

{ VITAMIN-PACKED FOR BONE, HEART & DIGESTIVE HEALTH }

1 c. kale (chopped and tightly packed)

1 ½ c. oat flour

1 ½ c. brown rice flour

½ c. pureed pumpkin (canned or fresh)

½ c. water (add slowly)

Preheat oven to 375°. Puree the kale in a food processor. Combine all ingredients (except the water) together. Add water slowly and mix until a dough forms (if too dry, add more water, too wet, add a bit more flour). You may not need all the water to reach the desired consistency. Use a cookie cutter (or a knife) to cut the dough into the desired shapes. Roll out on a lightly floured surface to ¼" thickness. Line a cookie sheet with parchment paper (for easy cleanup) and place the cookies on the sheet (they can be rather close together as they don't expand much while cooking).

Bake 18-25 minutes or until golden brown. Transfer and let cool completely on a wire rack. Store the cookies in an airtight container in the refrigerator. For more options, read the "Storage Tips" section on page 18.

BISON / ROSEMARY

{ A HEALTHIER RED MEAT OPTION, EASIER FOR DOGS WITH SENSITIVITIES TO BEEF }

1 ½ c. oat flour

1 ½ c. brown rice flour

½ c. ground bison (cooked)

2 tbsp. dried rosemary (ground)

1 egg

½ c. water (add slowly)

Preheat the oven to 350°. Combine all ingredients (except the water) together. Add water slowly and mix until a dough forms (if too dry, add more water, too wet, add a bit more flour). You may not need all the water to reach the desired consistency. Use a cookie cutter (or a knife) to cut the dough into the desired shapes. Roll out on a lightly floured surface to ¼" thickness. Line a cookie sheet with parchment paper (for easy cleanup) and place the cookies on the sheet (they can be rather close together as they don't expand much while cooking).

Bake 22-27 minutes or until golden brown. Transfer and let cool completely on a wire rack. Store the cookies in an airtight container in the refrigerator. For more options, read the "Storage Tips" section on page 18.

CAROB / PEANUT BUTTER

{ CAROB IS A HEALTHY ALTERNATIVE TO CHOCOLATE THAT'S TASTY & SAFE FOR DOGS }

1 ½ c. oat flour

1 ½ c. brown rice flour

½ c. peanut butter (unsalted, natural)

½ c. carob powder

1 egg

½ c. water (add slowly)

Preheat the oven to 375°. Combine all ingredients (except the water) together. Add water slowly and mix until a dough forms (if too dry, add more water, too wet, add a bit more flour). You may not need all the water to reach the desired consistency. Use a cookie cutter (or a knife) to cut the dough into the desired shapes. Roll out on a lightly floured surface to ¼" thickness. Line a cookie sheet with parchment paper (for easy cleanup) and place the cookies on the sheet (they can be rather close together as they don't expand much while cooking).

Bake 18-25 minutes or until golden brown. Transfer and let cool completely on a wire rack. Store the cookies in an airtight container in the refrigerator. For more options, read the "Storage Tips" section on page 18.

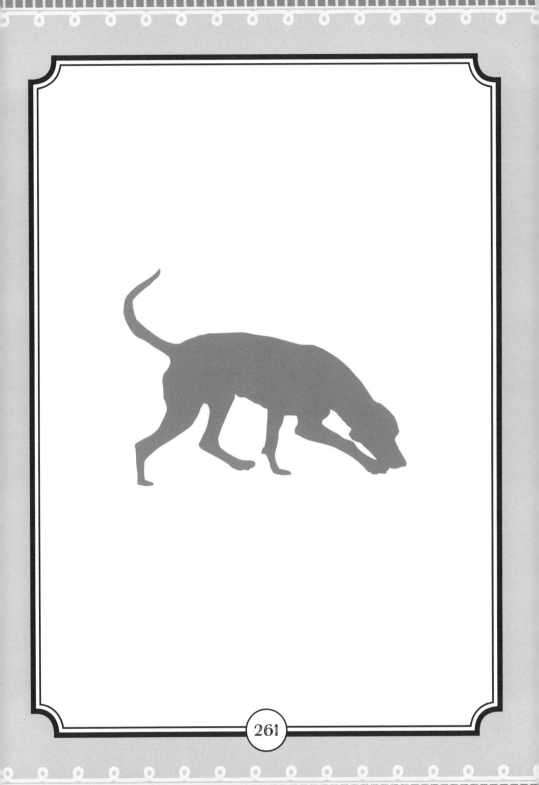

{ CHAPTER 9 }

FROZEN TREATS

For those warm summer days (and nights)

This collection of simple, quick, no-cook treats are the fastest and easiest ways to keep your pup busy on a warm summer day. The best part is they require no baking—yes, that's right! Just an ice cube or popsicle tray (small paper cups will also work) and you can make your dog their very own frosty treat, free from preservatives and full of healthy, beneficial ingredients.

FROZEN
STRAWBERRY / BANANA

{ COLD, REFRESHING & FULL OF VITAMINS }

....

1 c. pureed strawberries (fresh or frozen)

1 large banana (mashed and pureed)

1 c. plain nonfat yogurt

1 c. coconut water

Combine all ingredients together and whisk thoroughly. Pour mixture into an ice cube or popsicle tray. Freeze until solid (at least 4 hours).

FROZEN CHICKEN SOUP

{ GREAT SAVORY TASTE }

2 ½ c. chicken broth

½ c. carrots (shredded)

½ c. peas (frozen or canned)

1 tsp. ground parsley

Combine all ingredients together and whisk thoroughly. Pour mixture into an ice cube or popsicle tray. Freeze until solid (at least 4 hours).

FROZEN BLUEBERRY / OATS

{ DOGS DESERVE THEIR OWN ANTIOXIDANT-RICH FROZEN YOGURT TREAT }

1 c. blueberries (fresh or frozen)

½ c. old-fashioned rolled oats

2 c. plain nonfat yogurt

Combine all ingredients together and stir thoroughly. Pour mixture into an ice cube or popsicle tray. Freeze until solid (at least 4 hours).

Note: These make a great party favor for your next outing at the dog park.

FROZEN
PEANUT BUTTER / BACON

{ ASK YOUR PUP: IS THERE A TASTIER COMBO THAN BACON AND PEANUT BUTTER? }

4 slices bacon (cooked)

½ c. peanut butter (unsalted, natural)

2 c. plain nonfat yogurt

Finely chop the bacon. Combine all ingredients together and stir thoroughly. Pour mixture into an ice cube or popsicle tray. Freeze until solid (at least 4 hours).

FROZEN WATERMELON POPSICLE

{ PERFECT FOR THAT SUMMER BBQ OR DAY AT THE DOG PARK }

2 c. fresh watermelon (cubed)

1 c. coconut water

¼ c. flax seeds

⟶≫⟶•⟵≪⟵

Put all ingredients in a blender and mix until smooth. Pour mixture into an ice cube or popsicle tray. Freeze until solid (at least 4 hours).

Note: Make these extra special by inserting your dog's favorite biscuit or chewable into the wells of the ice cube tray. Then these little doggy ice pops will have the full effect.

FROZEN PEANUT BUTTER / BANANA SMOOTHIE

{ QUICK, EASY AND SURE TO PLEASE ANY DOG }

¹/₂ c. peanut butter (unsalted, natural)

1 ripe medium banana (mashed)

2 c. plain nonfat yogurt

Combine all ingredients together and stir thoroughly. Pour mixture into an ice cube or popsicle tray. Freeze until solid (at least 4 hours).

FROZEN BONE BROTH / TURMERIC / FLAX SEED

{ THIS IS A SUPERFOOD DELIGHT FOR YOUR PUP }

2 c. bone broth (beef, pork or poultry)

$^1/_2$ tsp. turmeric

1 tbsp. flaxseeds

Combine all ingredients together and stir thoroughly. Pour mixture into an ice cube or popsicle tray. Freeze until solid (at least 4 hours).

Note: Best enjoyed outside, or you can put the treat in their food bowl, so you don't end up with thawed bone broth on your floor.

FROZEN CRANBERRY / ALMOND / COCONUT

{ REFRESHING AND FILLED WITH PROTEIN, THIS ONE'S A WINNER }

....

2 c. plain nonfat yogurt

½ c. dried cranberries

½ c. almond butter (unsalted, natural)

1 c. coconut water

⟶⟩⟩⟩⟩—•—⟨⟨⟨⟵

Combine all ingredients together and stir thoroughly. Pour mixture into an ice cube or popsicle tray. Freeze until solid (at least 4 hours).

FROZEN BERRY PUPSICLES

{ CHOCK-FULL OF VITAMINS & ANTIOXIDANTS, THIS IS A CROWD PLEASER }

½ c. blueberries (fresh or frozen)

½ c. strawberries (finely chopped)

½ c. dried cranberries

2 c. plain nonfat yogurt

Combine all ingredients together and stir thoroughly. Pour mixture into an ice cube or popsicle tray. Freeze until solid (at least 4 hours).

Note: Make these extra special by inserting your dog's favorite biscuit or chew into each well of the ice cube tray. Then these little doggy pupsicles will have everyone wanting seconds.

FROZEN PUMPKIN /
PEANUT BUTTER STUFFER

{ KEEP YOUR DOG BUSY FOR HOURS WITH THIS TASTY FROZEN TREAT }

½ c. peanut butter (unsalted, natural)

½ c. pureed pumpkin (canned or fresh)

2 c. plain nonfat yogurt

Combine all ingredients together and stir thoroughly. Pour mixture into a kong or marrow bone. Freeze until solid (at least 4 hours).

Note: This is a great one to give your dog when you leave and put them in their crate. Or if you're having company over and want to keep them busy. It's healthy and they'll love you for it.

RESOURCES

There are thousands of websites of interest to dog owners these days, and the number of books on natural care continues to grow, too (how fortunate for us and our dogs!). We've been to quite a few of the sites and read lots of books, and this is our list of recommendations.

{ BOOKS ON NUTRITION }

Holistic Guide for a Healthy Dog, *by Wendy Volhard and Kerry Brown (Howell Book House, 2000)*

Dr. Pitcarin's New Complete Guide to Natural Health for Dogs and Cats, *by Richard H. Pitcairn and Susan Hubble Pitcairn (Rodale, 2005)*

The Goldsteins' Wellness & Longevity Program: Natural Care for Dogs and Cats, *by Robert S. Goldstein, VMD, and Susan Goldstein (TFH Publications, 2005)*

{ INTERNET REFERENCE SITES }

www.aspca.org
A wealth of information, including a list of substances that are poisonous to animals.

www.vet.cornell.library/publicsvcs/freeresources.cfm
A reliable network of informative websites and articles on all aspects of animal care, nutrition, behavior, disease, and so on.

RECIPE INDEX

SIDEBAR INDEX

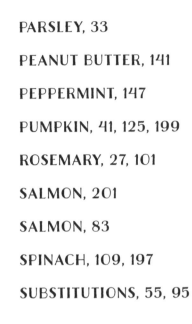

{ ABOUT CIDER MILL PRESS }

Good ideas ripen with time. From seed to harvest, Cider Mill Press brings fine reading, information, and entertainment together between the covers of its creatively crafted books. Our Cider Mill bears fruit twice a year, publishing a new crop of titles each spring and fall.

Where good books
are ready for press

VISIT US ON THE WEB AT
www.cidermillpress.com

OR WRITE TO US AT
PO Box 454
Kennebunkport, Maine 04046

{ ABOUT BUBBA ROSE BISCUIT CO. }

The Bubba Rose Biscuit Co. is the foremost purveyor of exceptionally crafted 5-star dog treats, with a selection as diverse as the breeds that love them. Bubba Rose was founded in 2006 by Jessica Disbrow, inspired by her rescue dogs Bob (aka Bubba) and Rose.

We bake our treats in small batches in our Miami, FL bakery—much like you will do with the recipes in this book. Our dog treats are delicious, attractive, and healthy—without preservatives, wheat, corn, soy, chemicals, sugar, salt, artificial flavors, colors, or fillers. What *is* in our treats? Nothing but human-grade US ingredients. Our meats and eggs are free-range, grain- and/or grass-fed, and free of antibiotics, added hormones, and nitrites.

Inspired by Bob and Rose, we are fully committed to helping make sure every dog gets a loving home to call their own. A portion of every Bubba Rose sale goes the Bubba Rose Foundation, Inc., our very own 501(c)3 non-profit to help the local stray population. Bubba Rose products are sold at over 1,200 locations nationwide and internationally. A media favorite, Jessica has been featured on the *Today Show*, HGTV's *Posh Pets*, NatGeo Wild's *Spoiled Rotten Pets*, and in *People*, *Country Living*, *Town & Country*, and *The Bark* magazines.

Bubba Rose
BISCUIT COMPANY

VISIT US AT **www.bubbarose.com**